RECLAIM. PIECE X PEACE

Vol: One Signature Edition

THIS JOURNAL BELONGS TO

_____

Dedicated To Those Who Are Ready To Set Their Souls Free

-Tatiana Jerome

TABLE OF CONTENTS

INTRODUCTION

I write to set my thoughts free. I write because I choose to create, break, and set records as well as destroy with my words. It's with the word that things come alive. It's with the written word as well as the spoken word that life takes its course. My word is one of the most powerful gifts God has given me as I know that in the beginning was the word and the word was with God and the word was God.

This is your time to set yourself free. Do it with your words. Use your words for truth, to break through barriers and to express who you truly are. Be aware that no one can tell your story better than you.

This journal is to be used to not only guide you through the healing process of a break up, but as a remembrance of what you are overcoming and who you are becoming. This is not just a record of a difficult place in your life but a journey through a challenging place that is propelling you towards a much healthier, inspired and loveable you.

You are being asked to use this journal as a place of peace. Leave everything on the page. Honor your feelings. Move accordingly with your words. Set the tone for your life. Even when there are days that you can do nothing but cry. . . Write. Even when there are days you can do nothing but rejoice. . . Write. Do not only write a good word but live within your words that you speak upon yourself. You will find that as you create with your words daily with this journal, you will gain strength to take action and view your life differently.

Imagine your new healed and healthy life with the new words you create. Imagine your next relationship with the words you create. Whatever you write, speak and focus upon in alignment with the word of God will come true when you believe. Your word is the steering wheel for the direction you are heading in and your beliefs are the engine

that powers your word. I created this journal for you to use towards the healing of your soul. As part of the Set In Soul Collection. . .it's now time to set your soul free.
I can't wait for you to feel amazing, alive and healed.

There is no such thing as coincidence as this was truly created and intended for you.

HOW TO USE THIS JOURNAL

Be honest with every question, every statement and every feeling. What you believe you were unable to express to your friends, family, your ex or even yourself at the time you were experiencing pain, you can now express here. Just like my book Love Lost Love Found, this journal is to guide you from your why this happened, to your what happens now. It's time to dig deep and answer the questions you have been avoiding (or wondering) about with clarity.

There are three sections within this journal. Each section has its own purpose and questions to get you to the next section and ultimately move you forward towards healing. Each section covers sixty days. That is a total of one hundred and eighty days. Each sixty days gives you the opportunity to not only break unwanted habits but to create and affirm some new ones.

I highly recommend that you use this journal daily. You may start whenever you like. Every morning after prayer (or whatever morning routine you practice), spend fifteen to twenty minutes answering your morning questions.

Fifteen to twenty minutes before your bedtime routine, spend some time answering the nightly questions. At first it may feel easy to do as you may have so many things that you've been wanting to express within you. But as you heal and get better, you will find that you will come to the journal not to vent but to declare and imagine your life in a much different space.

The main idea is to be absolutely truthful to you. If you are hurt, express that. If you feel resentment, let it be known. Each day as you get better in the art of expressing a piece of you, you will find that you are more than what tried to break you. You will begin to place more value towards the light that God has gifted within you.

REVELATIONS

ABOUT YOUR PREVIOUS RELATIONSHIP

Date: Current Mood:

Why did your previous relationship end?

Who ended the previous relationship?

Where did the previous relationship go wrong?

Who do you blame for the break up?

How could this break up have been avoided? Would you have been happy with that action?

Could whatever that ended the previous relationship have been worked out?

Did you and your previous partner try to work on the problem?

Was there infidelity within your previous relationship?

What did your previous partner say or do that you did not understand the purpose of?

What are your complaints about your previous partner?

Did your previous partner ignore you?

Did your previous partner respect you?

Did your previous partner treat you kindly?

Did your previous partner show affection towards you?

Could you and your previous partner handle heavy topics?

Did both of you know how to heal after a heavy conversation?

Did both of you know how to heal after being upset with each other?

Did you take your previous partner seriously? Why or why not?

Do you believe that your previous partner took you seriously? Why or why not?

Did you or your partner use the 'fear of intimacy' or the 'fear of commitment' as an excuse for unwanted behavior?

Were you or your previous partner passive about issues?

Did you or your previous partner try to keep things light to avoid issues?

What are some positive and negative words you would use to describe your previous partner?

Did you feel your previous partner could truly express themselves?

Could your previous partner be honest with you?

Do you believe your previous partner handled problems by hiding and running away?

Were there too many wrongs that needed to be made right before you could truly respect your previous partner?

If sex was involved, did you or your previous partner confuse sex for love?

INTROSPECTION

Did you feel that you were controlling in your previous relationship?

Did you obsess over your previous partner's every move?

Did you trust your previous partner?

Did you feel neglected in your previous relationship? Why?

Did you feel rejected in your previous relationship? Why?

When did you feel that you and your previous partner disconnected?

Why do you feel that you and your previous partner were disconnected?

Were you being true to your beliefs while in your previous relationships?

Could your previous partner handle talking about a future together?

Could you handle your previous partner talking about a future together?

Do you believe that you are 'needy' in your relationships?

Do you need constant reassurance in your relationships?

Did you feel that you could express yourself in your previous relationship?

Could you be honest with your previous partner?

Did you feel any changes in your previous relationship before you started to actually see them?

Did you ignore the warning signals of things going wrong in your previous relationship?

Did you ever address the warning signals? What were the results of you addressing them?

What hurts the most about the dissolve of your previous relationship?

Were you truly happy with your previous relationship?

Did you truly believe the previous relationship would last forever?

Were you able to be yourself in your previous relationship?

Do you regret anything about your previous relationship?

Did your previous partner help you to grow spiritually, mentally and/or emotionally while in your relationship?

What do you take personal accountability for?

What did you learn from your previous relationship?

If you could tell your previous partner anything right now, what would it be?

Did you stay in your previous relationship because you are comfortable?

Do you handle your problems by hiding and running away?

SECTION: 1

IT TRIED TO DESTROY ME

ABOUT THIS SECTION

This section will walk you through your first sixty days of healing. The best way to use this section is to spend the first few minutes within your morning filling out your morning thoughts. Be sure to let it all out. Where it states: Today I Affirm. . . state your affirmation. Write it down then repeat it to yourself for the next two minutes. Then write it down three more times within that section. Be sure to record the mood you woke up in, what you are going to do today to make yourself happy and more. Fill in as much as you can each day. If you cannot complete this within your morning, it is okay to revisit it throughout the day. It is recommended to carry this journal with you to remind yourself of the direction you are trying to move in.

Before you end your day, incorporate within your bedtime routine filling out the nightly questions. These questions are designed for introspection as well as preparation for the next day.

Each day is a new day with a chance to improve. It's not only a chance for the renewal of the mind and spirit, but it's also a chance to drop old habits as well as establish new ones. Remember that your focus should be on your wellbeing right now. While some days your thoughts and actions may not be perfect, it's okay. Your thoughts are adjusting for improvement. Any resistance you may feel is just a shifting into a new place that is trying to become your new normal. Time to get started.

MORNING THOUGHTS

Date:

Woke Up Feeling:

What Do I Need Help With Today:

Today I Affirm:

Today's Break Up Symptoms:

What Am I Doing Today To Make Me Happy?

Mood:

Today I Will Work On Thinking About?

Today I Want God To Know:

Today I Feel Tempted To:

The Reason Why I Will Not Do These Things Even If My Mind Tries To Rationalize it (Refer To Today I Feel Tempted To Question):

What I Wish To Say To My Ex Today:

NIGHTLY THOUGHTS

How Do I Currently Feel? Why?

Do I Feel Better Than Yesterday?

Did My Ex Try To Get My Attention By Communicating With Me Or Anyone I Know In Any Way?

What Song Best Describes My Mood?

Did I Do A Good Job Protecting My Space Today?

I Am Thankful For?

What Could I Have Done A Better Job At Today?

Today I Learned...

What Do I Look Forward To Tomorrow?

I Am Worthy Of:

Tatiana's Personal Note: Please remember that pain does not last forever.

MORNING THOUGHTS

Date:

Mood:

Woke Up Feeling:

Today I Will Work On Thinking About?

What Do I Need Help With Today:

Today I Want God To Know:

Today I Affirm:

Today I Feel Tempted To:

Today's Break Up Symptoms:

The Reason Why I Will Not Do These Things Even If My Mind Tries To Rationalize it (Refer To Today I Feel Tempted To Question):

What Am I Doing Today To Make Me Happy?

What I Wish To Say To My Ex Today:

NIGHTLY THOUGHTS

How Do I Currently Feel? Why?

Do I Feel Better Than Yesterday?

Did My Ex Try To Get My Attention By Communicating With Me Or Anyone I Know In Any Way?

What Song Best Describes My Mood?

Did I Do A Good Job Protecting My Space Today?

I Am Thankful For?

What Could I Have Done A Better Job At Today?

Today I Learned...

What Do I Look Forward To Tomorrow?

I Am Worthy Of:

Tatiana's Personal Note: Things fall apart for you to receive better.

MORNING THOUGHTS

Date:

Mood:

Woke Up Feeling:

Today I Will Work On Thinking About?

What Do I Need Help With Today:

Today I Want God To Know:

Today I Affirm:

Today I Feel Tempted To:

Today's Break Up Symptoms:

The Reason Why I Will Not Do These Things
Even If My Mind Tries To Rationalize it
(Refer To Today I Feel Tempted To Question):

What Am I Doing Today To Make Me Happy?

What I Wish To Say To My Ex Today:

NIGHTLY THOUGHTS

How Do I Currently Feel? Why?

Do I Feel Better Than Yesterday?

Did My Ex Try To Get My Attention By Communicating With Me Or Anyone I Know In Any Way?

What Song Best Describes My Mood?

Did I Do A Good Job Protecting My Space Today?

I Am Thankful For?

What Could I Have Done A Better Job At Today?

Today I Learned...

What Do I Look Forward To Tomorrow?

I Am Worthy Of:

Tatiana's Personal Note: You are overqualified to be holding on to someone underqualified.

WHAT I KNOW:
NO MORE STRUGGLING WITH WHAT I SETTLED FOR

MORNING THOUGHTS

Date:

Mood:

Woke Up Feeling:

Today I Will Work On Thinking About?

What Do I Need Help With Today:

Today I Want God To Know:

Today I Affirm:

Today I Feel Tempted To:

Today's Break Up Symptoms:

The Reason Why I Will Not Do These Things Even If My Mind Tries To Rationalize it (Refer To Today I Feel Tempted To Question):

What Am I Doing Today To Make Me Happy?

What I Wish To Say To My Ex Today:

NIGHTLY THOUGHTS

How Do I Currently Feel? Why?

Do I Feel Better Than Yesterday?

Did My Ex Try To Get My Attention By Communicating With Me Or Anyone I Know In Any Way?

What Song Best Describes My Mood?

Did I Do A Good Job Protecting My Space Today?

I Am Thankful For?

What Could I Have Done A Better Job At Today?

Today I Learned...

What Do I Look Forward To Tomorrow?

I Am Worthy Of:

Tatiana's Personal Note: The pain was not created to hurt you, but to create a stronger version of you.

MORNING THOUGHTS

Date:

Mood:

Woke Up Feeling:

Today I Will Work On Thinking About?

What Do I Need Help With Today:

Today I Want God To Know:

Today I Affirm:

Today I Feel Tempted To:

Today's Break Up Symptoms:

The Reason Why I Will Not Do These Things Even If My Mind Tries To Rationalize it (Refer To Today I Feel Tempted To Question):

What Am I Doing Today To Make Me Happy?

What I Wish To Say To My Ex Today:

NIGHTLY THOUGHTS

How Do I Currently Feel? Why?

Do I Feel Better Than Yesterday?

Did My Ex Try To Get My Attention By Communicating With Me Or Anyone I Know In Any Way?

What Song Best Describes My Mood?

Did I Do A Good Job Protecting My Space Today?

I Am Thankful For?

What Could I Have Done A Better Job At Today?

Today I Learned...

What Do I Look Forward To Tomorrow?

I Am Worthy Of:

Tatiana's Personal Note: The older I get the more I realize piece by piece I won't settle for anything that disturbs my peace.

MORNING THOUGHTS

Date:

Mood:

Woke Up Feeling:

Today I Will Work On Thinking About?

What Do I Need Help With Today:

Today I Want God To Know:

Today I Affirm:

Today I Feel Tempted To:

Today's Break Up Symptoms:

The Reason Why I Will Not Do These Things Even If My Mind Tries To Rationalize it (Refer To Today I Feel Tempted To Question):

What Am I Doing Today To Make Me Happy?

What I Wish To Say To My Ex Today:

NIGHTLY THOUGHTS

How Do I Currently Feel? Why?

Do I Feel Better Than Yesterday?

Did My Ex Try To Get My Attention By Communicating With Me Or Anyone I Know In Any Way?

What Song Best Describes My Mood?

Did I Do A Good Job Protecting My Space Today?

I Am Thankful For?

What Could I Have Done A Better Job At Today?

Today I Learned...

What Do I Look Forward To Tomorrow?

I Am Worthy Of:

Tatiana's Personal Note: Sometimes you have to let go to see what happens.

MORNING THOUGHTS

Date: Mood:

Woke Up Feeling: Today I Will Work On Thinking About?

What Do I Need Help With Today: Today I Want God To Know:

Today I Affirm: Today I Feel Tempted To:

Today's Break Up Symptoms: The Reason Why I Will Not Do These Things
                                                     Even If My Mind Tries To Rationalize it
                                                     (Refer To Today I Feel Tempted To Question):

What Am I Doing Today To Make Me Happy? What I Wish To Say To My Ex Today:

NIGHTLY THOUGHTS

How Do I Currently Feel? Why?

Do I Feel Better Than Yesterday?

Did My Ex Try To Get My Attention By Communicating With Me Or Anyone I Know In Any Way?

What Song Best Describes My Mood?

Did I Do A Good Job Protecting My Space Today?

I Am Thankful For?

What Could I Have Done A Better Job At Today?

Today I Learned...

What Do I Look Forward To Tomorrow?

I Am Worthy Of:

Tatiana's Personal Note: You are not created for everyone and only a special someone will understand that.

MORNING THOUGHTS

Date:

Mood:

Woke Up Feeling:

Today I Will Work On Thinking About?

What Do I Need Help With Today:

Today I Want God To Know:

Today I Affirm:

Today I Feel Tempted To:

Today's Break Up Symptoms:

The Reason Why I Will Not Do These Things
Even If My Mind Tries To Rationalize it
(Refer To Today I Feel Tempted To Question):

What Am I Doing Today To Make Me Happy?

What I Wish To Say To My Ex Today:

NIGHTLY THOUGHTS

How Do I Currently Feel? Why?

Do I Feel Better Than Yesterday?

Did My Ex Try To Get My Attention By Communicating With Me Or Anyone I Know In Any Way?

What Song Best Describes My Mood?

Did I Do A Good Job Protecting My Space Today?

I Am Thankful For?

What Could I Have Done A Better Job At Today?

Today I Learned...

What Do I Look Forward To Tomorrow?

I Am Worthy Of:

Tatiana's Personal Note: What you do not understand you will soon.

MORNING THOUGHTS

Date: Mood:

Woke Up Feeling: Today I Will Work On Thinking About?

What Do I Need Help With Today: Today I Want God To Know:

Today I Affirm: Today I Feel Tempted To:

Today's Break Up Symptoms: The Reason Why I Will Not Do These Things
                                               Even If My Mind Tries To Rationalize it
                                               (Refer To Today I Feel Tempted To Question):

What Am I Doing Today To Make Me Happy?   What I Wish To Say To My Ex Today:

NIGHTLY THOUGHTS

How Do I Currently Feel? Why?

Do I Feel Better Than Yesterday?

Did My Ex Try To Get My Attention By Communicating With Me Or Anyone I Know In Any Way?

What Song Best Describes My Mood?

Did I Do A Good Job Protecting My Space Today?

I Am Thankful For?

What Could I Have Done A Better Job At Today?

Today I Learned...

What Do I Look Forward To Tomorrow?

I Am Worthy Of:

Tatiana's Personal Note: Love is not confusing.

REMINDER TO SELF: IT FEELS GOOD TO BE RELEASED FROM CHAOS

I WOULD RATHER BE HONEST WITH MYSELF THAN LOSE MYSELF IN WHAT WAS NEVER FOR ME

- BECAUSE

MORNING THOUGHTS

Date:

Woke Up Feeling:

What Do I Need Help With Today:

Today I Affirm:

Today's Break Up Symptoms:

What Am I Doing Today To Make Me Happy?

Mood:

Today I Will Work On Thinking About?

Today I Want God To Know:

Today I Feel Tempted To:

The Reason Why I Will Not Do These Things
Even If My Mind Tries To Rationalize it
(Refer To Today I Feel Tempted To Question):

What I Wish To Say To My Ex Today:

NIGHTLY THOUGHTS

How Do I Currently Feel? Why?

Do I Feel Better Than Yesterday?

Did My Ex Try To Get My Attention By Communicating With Me Or Anyone I Know In Any Way?

What Song Best Describes My Mood?

Did I Do A Good Job Protecting My Space Today?

I Am Thankful For?

What Could I Have Done A Better Job At Today?

Today I Learned...

What Do I Look Forward To Tomorrow?

I Am Worthy Of:

Tatiana's Personal Note: I'll work for it. I'll pray for it. I won't force it to work.

45

MORNING THOUGHTS

Date: Mood:

Woke Up Feeling: Today I Will Work On Thinking About?

What Do I Need Help With Today: Today I Want God To Know:

Today I Affirm: Today I Feel Tempted To:

Today's Break Up Symptoms: The Reason Why I Will Not Do These Things
                                         Even If My Mind Tries To Rationalize it
                                         (Refer To Today I Feel Tempted To Question):

What Am I Doing Today To Make Me Happy?   What I Wish To Say To My Ex Today:

NIGHTLY THOUGHTS

How Do I Currently Feel? Why?

Do I Feel Better Than Yesterday?

Did My Ex Try To Get My Attention By Communicating With Me Or Anyone I Know In Any Way?

What Song Best Describes My Mood?

Did I Do A Good Job Protecting My Space Today?

I Am Thankful For?

What Could I Have Done A Better Job At Today?

Today I Learned...

What Do I Look Forward To Tomorrow?

I Am Worthy Of:

Tatiana's Personal Note: Stop getting offended by someone else's way of life.

MORNING THOUGHTS

Date:

Mood:

Woke Up Feeling:

Today I Will Work On Thinking About?

What Do I Need Help With Today:

Today I Want God To Know:

Today I Affirm:

Today I Feel Tempted To:

Today's Break Up Symptoms:

The Reason Why I Will Not Do These Things Even If My Mind Tries To Rationalize it (Refer To Today I Feel Tempted To Question):

What Am I Doing Today To Make Me Happy?

What I Wish To Say To My Ex Today:

NIGHTLY THOUGHTS

How Do I Currently Feel? Why?

Do I Feel Better Than Yesterday?

Did My Ex Try To Get My Attention By Communicating With Me Or Anyone I Know In Any Way?

What Song Best Describes My Mood?

Did I Do A Good Job Protecting My Space Today?

I Am Thankful For?

What Could I Have Done A Better Job At Today?

Today I Learned...

What Do I Look Forward To Tomorrow?

I Am Worthy Of:

Tatiana's Personal Note: Standards only scare off people not meant for you.

MORNING THOUGHTS

Date: Mood:

Woke Up Feeling: Today I Will Work On Thinking About?

What Do I Need Help With Today: Today I Want God To Know:

Today I Affirm: Today I Feel Tempted To:

Today's Break Up Symptoms: The Reason Why I Will Not Do These Things
                                                   Even If My Mind Tries To Rationalize it
                                                   (Refer To Today I Feel Tempted To Question):

What Am I Doing Today To Make Me Happy?   What I Wish To Say To My Ex Today:

NIGHTLY THOUGHTS

How Do I Currently Feel? Why?

Do I Feel Better Than Yesterday?

Did My Ex Try To Get My Attention By Communicating With Me Or Anyone I Know In Any Way?

What Song Best Describes My Mood?

Did I Do A Good Job Protecting My Space Today?

I Am Thankful For?

What Could I Have Done A Better Job At Today?

Today I Learned...

What Do I Look Forward To Tomorrow?

I Am Worthy Of:

Tatiana's Personal Note: Your happiness should not be up for negotiation.

MORNING THOUGHTS

Date:

Mood:

Woke Up Feeling:

Today I Will Work On Thinking About?

What Do I Need Help With Today:

Today I Want God To Know:

Today I Affirm:

Today I Feel Tempted To:

Today's Break Up Symptoms:

The Reason Why I Will Not Do These Things
Even If My Mind Tries To Rationalize it
(Refer To Today I Feel Tempted To Question):

What Am I Doing Today To Make Me Happy?

What I Wish To Say To My Ex Today:

NIGHTLY THOUGHTS

How Do I Currently Feel? Why?

Do I Feel Better Than Yesterday?

Did My Ex Try To Get My Attention By Communicating With Me Or Anyone I Know In Any Way?

What Song Best Describes My Mood?

Did I Do A Good Job Protecting My Space Today?

I Am Thankful For?

What Could I Have Done A Better Job At Today?

Today I Learned...

What Do I Look Forward To Tomorrow?

I Am Worthy Of:

Tatiana's Personal Note: You cannot change others, nor should you want to.

MORNING THOUGHTS

Date:

Mood:

Woke Up Feeling:

Today I Will Work On Thinking About?

What Do I Need Help With Today:

Today I Want God To Know:

Today I Affirm:

Today I Feel Tempted To:

Today's Break Up Symptoms:

The Reason Why I Will Not Do These Things
Even If My Mind Tries To Rationalize it
(Refer To Today I Feel Tempted To Question):

What Am I Doing Today To Make Me Happy?

What I Wish To Say To My Ex Today:

NIGHTLY THOUGHTS

How Do I Currently Feel? Why?

Do I Feel Better Than Yesterday?

Did My Ex Try To Get My Attention By Communicating With Me Or Anyone I Know In Any Way?

What Song Best Describes My Mood?

Did I Do A Good Job Protecting My Space Today?

I Am Thankful For?

What Could I Have Done A Better Job At Today?

Today I Learned...

What Do I Look Forward To Tomorrow?

I Am Worthy Of:

Tatiana's Personal Note: Be aware of your value.

MORNING THOUGHTS

Date:

Mood:

Woke Up Feeling:

Today I Will Work On Thinking About?

What Do I Need Help With Today:

Today I Want God To Know:

Today I Affirm:

Today I Feel Tempted To:

Today's Break Up Symptoms:

The Reason Why I Will Not Do These Things Even If My Mind Tries To Rationalize it (Refer To Today I Feel Tempted To Question):

What Am I Doing Today To Make Me Happy?

What I Wish To Say To My Ex Today:

NIGHTLY THOUGHTS

How Do I Currently Feel? Why?

Do I Feel Better Than Yesterday?

Did My Ex Try To Get My Attention By Communicating With Me Or Anyone I Know In Any Way?

What Song Best Describes My Mood?

Did I Do A Good Job Protecting My Space Today?

I Am Thankful For?

What Could I Have Done A Better Job At Today?

Today I Learned...

What Do I Look Forward To Tomorrow?

I Am Worthy Of:

Tatiana's Personal Note: Learn to accept what is. Accept where you are.

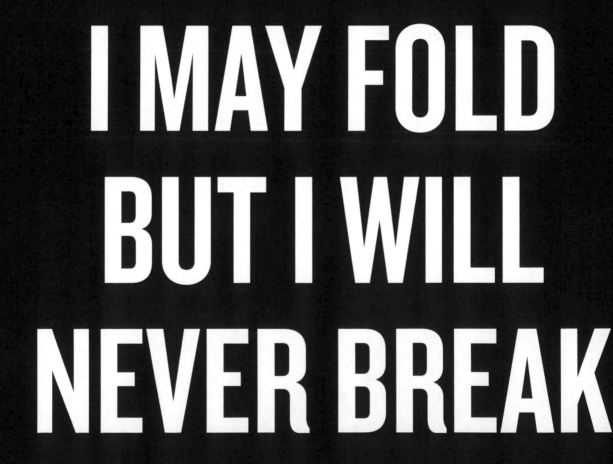

THERE IS NOTHING WRONG WITH VULNERABILITY

MORNING THOUGHTS

Date:

Woke Up Feeling:

What Do I Need Help With Today:

Today I Affirm:

Today's Break Up Symptoms:

What Am I Doing Today To Make Me Happy?

Mood:

Today I Will Work On Thinking About?

Today I Want God To Know:

Today I Feel Tempted To:

The Reason Why I Will Not Do These Things
Even If My Mind Tries To Rationalize it
(Refer To Today I Feel Tempted To Question):

What I Wish To Say To My Ex Today:

NIGHTLY THOUGHTS

How Do I Currently Feel? Why?

Do I Feel Better Than Yesterday?

Did My Ex Try To Get My Attention By Communicating With Me Or Anyone I Know In Any Way?

What Song Best Describes My Mood?

Did I Do A Good Job Protecting My Space Today?

I Am Thankful For?

What Could I Have Done A Better Job At Today?

Today I Learned...

What Do I Look Forward To Tomorrow?

I Am Worthy Of:

Tatiana's Personal Note: Love does not create excuses.

VALUING EVERYTHING THEY DID NOT VALUE ABOUT ME

GOD IS MY
BEST FRIEND

MORNING THOUGHTS

Date:

Mood:

Woke Up Feeling:

Today I Will Work On Thinking About?

What Do I Need Help With Today:

Today I Want God To Know:

Today I Affirm:

Today I Feel Tempted To:

Today's Break Up Symptoms:

The Reason Why I Will Not Do These Things Even If My Mind Tries To Rationalize it (Refer To Today I Feel Tempted To Question):

What Am I Doing Today To Make Me Happy?

What I Wish To Say To My Ex Today:

NIGHTLY THOUGHTS

How Do I Currently Feel? Why?

Do I Feel Better Than Yesterday?

Did My Ex Try To Get My Attention By Communicating With Me Or Anyone I Know In Any Way?

What Song Best Describes My Mood?

Did I Do A Good Job Protecting My Space Today?

I Am Thankful For?

What Could I Have Done A Better Job At Today?

Today I Learned...

What Do I Look Forward To Tomorrow?

I Am Worthy Of:

Tatiana's Personal Note: You will never catch what keeps running away so stop chasing.

MORNING THOUGHTS

Date:

Mood:

Woke Up Feeling:

Today I Will Work On Thinking About?

What Do I Need Help With Today:

Today I Want God To Know:

Today I Affirm:

Today I Feel Tempted To:

Today's Break Up Symptoms:

The Reason Why I Will Not Do These Things
Even If My Mind Tries To Rationalize it
(Refer To Today I Feel Tempted To Question):

What Am I Doing Today To Make Me Happy?

What I Wish To Say To My Ex Today:

NIGHTLY THOUGHTS

How Do I Currently Feel? Why?

Do I Feel Better Than Yesterday?

Did My Ex Try To Get My Attention By Communicating With Me Or Anyone I Know In Any Way?

What Song Best Describes My Mood?

Did I Do A Good Job Protecting My Space Today?

I Am Thankful For?

What Could I Have Done A Better Job At Today?

Today I Learned...

What Do I Look Forward To Tomorrow?

I Am Worthy Of:

Tatiana's Personal Note: Your biggest blessing may come from your biggest disappointments.

MORNING THOUGHTS

Date:

Mood:

Woke Up Feeling:

Today I Will Work On Thinking About?

What Do I Need Help With Today:

Today I Want God To Know:

Today I Affirm:

Today I Feel Tempted To:

Today's Break Up Symptoms:

The Reason Why I Will Not Do These Things
Even If My Mind Tries To Rationalize it
(Refer To Today I Feel Tempted To Question):

What Am I Doing Today To Make Me Happy?

What I Wish To Say To My Ex Today:

NIGHTLY THOUGHTS

How Do I Currently Feel? Why?

Do I Feel Better Than Yesterday?

Did My Ex Try To Get My Attention By Communicating With Me Or Anyone I Know In Any Way?

What Song Best Describes My Mood?

Did I Do A Good Job Protecting My Space Today?

I Am Thankful For?

What Could I Have Done A Better Job At Today?

Today I Learned...

What Do I Look Forward To Tomorrow?

I Am Worthy Of:

Tatiana's Personal Note: Accept the apology you may never get.

MORNING THOUGHTS

Date:

Mood:

Woke Up Feeling:

Today I Will Work On Thinking About?

What Do I Need Help With Today:

Today I Want God To Know:

Today I Affirm:

Today I Feel Tempted To:

Today's Break Up Symptoms:

The Reason Why I Will Not Do These Things
Even If My Mind Tries To Rationalize it
(Refer To Today I Feel Tempted To Question):

What Am I Doing Today To Make Me Happy?

What I Wish To Say To My Ex Today:

NIGHTLY THOUGHTS

How Do I Currently Feel? Why?

Do I Feel Better Than Yesterday?

Did My Ex Try To Get My Attention By Communicating With Me Or Anyone I Know In Any Way?

What Song Best Describes My Mood?

Did I Do A Good Job Protecting My Space Today?

I Am Thankful For?

What Could I Have Done A Better Job At Today?

Today I Learned...

What Do I Look Forward To Tomorrow?

I Am Worthy Of:

Tatiana's Personal Note: Anything that is true will commit.

MORNING THOUGHTS

Date:

Mood:

Woke Up Feeling:

Today I Will Work On Thinking About?

What Do I Need Help With Today:

Today I Want God To Know:

Today I Affirm:

Today I Feel Tempted To:

Today's Break Up Symptoms:

The Reason Why I Will Not Do These Things
Even If My Mind Tries To Rationalize it
(Refer To Today I Feel Tempted To Question):

What Am I Doing Today To Make Me Happy?

What I Wish To Say To My Ex Today:

NIGHTLY THOUGHTS

How Do I Currently Feel? Why?

Do I Feel Better Than Yesterday?

Did My Ex Try To Get My Attention By Communicating With Me Or Anyone I Know In Any Way?

What Song Best Describes My Mood?

Did I Do A Good Job Protecting My Space Today?

I Am Thankful For?

What Could I Have Done A Better Job At Today?

Today I Learned...

What Do I Look Forward To Tomorrow?

I Am Worthy Of:

Tatiana's Personal Note: Life can change in a minute.

MORNING THOUGHTS

Date:

Woke Up Feeling:

What Do I Need Help With Today:

Today I Affirm:

Today's Break Up Symptoms:

What Am I Doing Today To Make Me Happy?

Mood:

Today I Will Work On Thinking About?

Today I Want God To Know:

Today I Feel Tempted To:

The Reason Why I Will Not Do These Things
Even If My Mind Tries To Rationalize it
(Refer To Today I Feel Tempted To Question):

What I Wish To Say To My Ex Today:

NIGHTLY THOUGHTS

How Do I Currently Feel? Why?

Do I Feel Better Than Yesterday?

Did My Ex Try To Get My Attention By Communicating With Me Or Anyone I Know In Any Way?

What Song Best Describes My Mood?

Did I Do A Good Job Protecting My Space Today?

I Am Thankful For?

What Could I Have Done A Better Job At Today?

Today I Learned...

What Do I Look Forward To Tomorrow?

I Am Worthy Of:

Tatiana's Personal Note: Your future is in God's hands.

MORNING THOUGHTS

Date:

Mood:

Woke Up Feeling:

Today I Will Work On Thinking About?

What Do I Need Help With Today:

Today I Want God To Know:

Today I Affirm:

Today I Feel Tempted To:

Today's Break Up Symptoms:

The Reason Why I Will Not Do These Things
Even If My Mind Tries To Rationalize it
(Refer To Today I Feel Tempted To Question):

What Am I Doing Today To Make Me Happy?

What I Wish To Say To My Ex Today:

NIGHTLY THOUGHTS

How Do I Currently Feel? Why?

Do I Feel Better Than Yesterday?

Did My Ex Try To Get My Attention By Communicating With Me Or Anyone I Know In Any Way?

What Song Best Describes My Mood?

Did I Do A Good Job Protecting My Space Today?

I Am Thankful For?

What Could I Have Done A Better Job At Today?

Today I Learned...

What Do I Look Forward To Tomorrow?

I Am Worthy Of:

Tatiana's Personal Note: You are strong and can have and do anything. Be a believer.

MORNING THOUGHTS

Date: Mood:

Woke Up Feeling: Today I Will Work On Thinking About?

What Do I Need Help With Today: Today I Want God To Know:

Today I Affirm: Today I Feel Tempted To:

Today's Break Up Symptoms: The Reason Why I Will Not Do These Things
                                           Even If My Mind Tries To Rationalize it
                                           (Refer To Today I Feel Tempted To Question):

What Am I Doing Today To Make Me Happy?   What I Wish To Say To My Ex Today:

NIGHTLY THOUGHTS

How Do I Currently Feel? Why?

Did My Ex Try To Get My Attention By Communicating With Me Or Anyone I Know In Any Way?

Did I Do A Good Job Protecting My Space Today?

What Could I Have Done A Better Job At Today?

What Do I Look Forward To Tomorrow?

Do I Feel Better Than Yesterday?

What Song Best Describes My Mood?

I Am Thankful For?

Today I Learned...

I Am Worthy Of:

Tatiana's Personal Note: Know what you deserve.

MORNING THOUGHTS

Date:

Woke Up Feeling:

What Do I Need Help With Today:

Today I Affirm:

Today's Break Up Symptoms:

What Am I Doing Today To Make Me Happy?

Mood:

Today I Will Work On Thinking About?

Today I Want God To Know:

Today I Feel Tempted To:

The Reason Why I Will Not Do These Things Even If My Mind Tries To Rationalize it (Refer To Today I Feel Tempted To Question):

What I Wish To Say To My Ex Today:

NIGHTLY THOUGHTS

How Do I Currently Feel? Why?

Do I Feel Better Than Yesterday?

Did My Ex Try To Get My Attention By Communicating With Me Or Anyone I Know In Any Way?

What Song Best Describes My Mood?

Did I Do A Good Job Protecting My Space Today?

I Am Thankful For?

What Could I Have Done A Better Job At Today?

Today I Learned...

What Do I Look Forward To Tomorrow?

I Am Worthy Of:

Tatiana's Personal Note: It is okay to make mistakes …. as long as you grow from them.

MORNING THOUGHTS

Date: Mood:

Woke Up Feeling: Today I Will Work On Thinking About?

What Do I Need Help With Today: Today I Want God To Know:

Today I Affirm: Today I Feel Tempted To:

Today's Break Up Symptoms: The Reason Why I Will Not Do These Things
                                                   Even If My Mind Tries To Rationalize it
                                                   (Refer To Today I Feel Tempted To Question):

What Am I Doing Today To Make Me Happy?   What I Wish To Say To My Ex Today:

NIGHTLY THOUGHTS

How Do I Currently Feel? Why?

Do I Feel Better Than Yesterday?

Did My Ex Try To Get My Attention By Communicating With Me Or Anyone I Know In Any Way?

What Song Best Describes My Mood?

Did I Do A Good Job Protecting My Space Today?

I Am Thankful For?

What Could I Have Done A Better Job At Today?

Today I Learned...

What Do I Look Forward To Tomorrow?

I Am Worthy Of:

Tatiana's Personal Note: Love when you are hurting. Love when you are happy.

MORNING THOUGHTS

Date:

Woke Up Feeling:

What Do I Need Help With Today:

Today I Affirm:

Today's Break Up Symptoms:

What Am I Doing Today To Make Me Happy?

Mood:

Today I Will Work On Thinking About?

Today I Want God To Know:

Today I Feel Tempted To:

The Reason Why I Will Not Do These Things
Even If My Mind Tries To Rationalize it
(Refer To Today I Feel Tempted To Question):

What I Wish To Say To My Ex Today:

NIGHTLY THOUGHTS

How Do I Currently Feel? Why?

Do I Feel Better Than Yesterday?

Did My Ex Try To Get My Attention By Communicating With Me Or Anyone I Know In Any Way?

What Song Best Describes My Mood?

Did I Do A Good Job Protecting My Space Today?

I Am Thankful For?

What Could I Have Done A Better Job At Today?

Today I Learned...

What Do I Look Forward To Tomorrow?

I Am Worthy Of:

Tatiana's Personal Note: It is how you deal with your imperfections that makes you perfect.

MORNING THOUGHTS

Date:

Woke Up Feeling:

What Do I Need Help With Today:

Today I Affirm:

Today's Break Up Symptoms:

What Am I Doing Today To Make Me Happy?

Mood:

Today I Will Work On Thinking About?

Today I Want God To Know:

Today I Feel Tempted To:

The Reason Why I Will Not Do These Things
Even If My Mind Tries To Rationalize it
(Refer To Today I Feel Tempted To Question):

What I Wish To Say To My Ex Today:

NIGHTLY THOUGHTS

How Do I Currently Feel? Why?

Do I Feel Better Than Yesterday?

Did My Ex Try To Get My Attention By Communicating With Me Or Anyone I Know In Any Way?

What Song Best Describes My Mood?

Did I Do A Good Job Protecting My Space Today?

I Am Thankful For?

What Could I Have Done A Better Job At Today?

Today I Learned...

What Do I Look Forward To Tomorrow?

I Am Worthy Of:

Tatiana's Personal Note: Never feel guilty for doing what's best for you.

MY HEART MAY BE HURTING BUT IT'S FORGIVING

EVERYTHING IS FALLING INTO PLACE. EVERYTHING.

MORNING THOUGHTS

Date:

Mood:

Woke Up Feeling:

Today I Will Work On Thinking About?

What Do I Need Help With Today:

Today I Want God To Know:

Today I Affirm:

Today I Feel Tempted To:

Today's Break Up Symptoms:

The Reason Why I Will Not Do These Things Even If My Mind Tries To Rationalize it (Refer To Today I Feel Tempted To Question):

What Am I Doing Today To Make Me Happy?

What I Wish To Say To My Ex Today:

NIGHTLY THOUGHTS

How Do I Currently Feel? Why?

Do I Feel Better Than Yesterday?

Did My Ex Try To Get My Attention By Communicating With Me Or Anyone I Know In Any Way?

What Song Best Describes My Mood?

Did I Do A Good Job Protecting My Space Today?

I Am Thankful For?

What Could I Have Done A Better Job At Today?

Today I Learned...

What Do I Look Forward To Tomorrow?

I Am Worthy Of:

Tatiana's Personal Note: What you overcome is what brings you closer to who you have prayed to become.

MORNING THOUGHTS

Date: | Mood:

Woke Up Feeling: | Today I Will Work On Thinking About?

What Do I Need Help With Today: | Today I Want God To Know:

Today I Affirm: | Today I Feel Tempted To:

Today's Break Up Symptoms: | The Reason Why I Will Not Do These Things
                                               | Even If My Mind Tries To Rationalize it
                                               | (Refer To Today I Feel Tempted To Question):

What Am I Doing Today To Make Me Happy? | What I Wish To Say To My Ex Today:

NIGHTLY THOUGHTS

How Do I Currently Feel? Why?

Do I Feel Better Than Yesterday?

Did My Ex Try To Get My Attention By Communicating With Me Or Anyone I Know In Any Way?

What Song Best Describes My Mood?

Did I Do A Good Job Protecting My Space Today?

I Am Thankful For?

What Could I Have Done A Better Job At Today?

Today I Learned...

What Do I Look Forward To Tomorrow?

I Am Worthy Of:

Tatiana's Personal Note: You are beauty.

MORNING THOUGHTS

Date:

Mood:

Woke Up Feeling:

Today I Will Work On Thinking About?

What Do I Need Help With Today:

Today I Want God To Know:

Today I Affirm:

Today I Feel Tempted To:

Today's Break Up Symptoms:

The Reason Why I Will Not Do These Things
Even If My Mind Tries To Rationalize it
(Refer To Today I Feel Tempted To Question):

What Am I Doing Today To Make Me Happy?

What I Wish To Say To My Ex Today:

NIGHTLY THOUGHTS

How Do I Currently Feel? Why?

Do I Feel Better Than Yesterday?

Did My Ex Try To Get My Attention By Communicating With Me Or Anyone I Know In Any Way?

What Song Best Describes My Mood?

Did I Do A Good Job Protecting My Space Today?

I Am Thankful For?

What Could I Have Done A Better Job At Today?

Today I Learned...

What Do I Look Forward To Tomorrow?

I Am Worthy Of:

Tatiana's Personal Note: Stillness will eliminate confusion.

MORNING THOUGHTS

Date: Mood:

Woke Up Feeling: Today I Will Work On Thinking About?

What Do I Need Help With Today: Today I Want God To Know:

Today I Affirm: Today I Feel Tempted To:

Today's Break Up Symptoms: The Reason Why I Will Not Do These Things
                                               Even If My Mind Tries To Rationalize it
                                               (Refer To Today I Feel Tempted To Question):

What Am I Doing Today To Make Me Happy?   What I Wish To Say To My Ex Today:

NIGHTLY THOUGHTS

How Do I Currently Feel? Why?

Do I Feel Better Than Yesterday?

Did My Ex Try To Get My Attention By Communicating With Me Or Anyone I Know In Any Way?

What Song Best Describes My Mood?

Did I Do A Good Job Protecting My Space Today?

I Am Thankful For?

What Could I Have Done A Better Job At Today?

Today I Learned...

What Do I Look Forward To Tomorrow?

I Am Worthy Of:

Tatiana's Personal Note: Sometimes you go through the worst times of your life to get to the best times.

MORNING THOUGHTS

Date:

Mood:

Woke Up Feeling:

Today I Will Work On Thinking About?

What Do I Need Help With Today:

Today I Want God To Know:

Today I Affirm:

Today I Feel Tempted To:

Today's Break Up Symptoms:

The Reason Why I Will Not Do These Things
Even If My Mind Tries To Rationalize it
(Refer To Today I Feel Tempted To Question):

What Am I Doing Today To Make Me Happy?

What I Wish To Say To My Ex Today:

NIGHTLY THOUGHTS

How Do I Currently Feel? Why?

Do I Feel Better Than Yesterday?

Did My Ex Try To Get My Attention By Communicating With Me Or Anyone I Know In Any Way?

What Song Best Describes My Mood?

Did I Do A Good Job Protecting My Space Today?

I Am Thankful For?

What Could I Have Done A Better Job At Today?

Today I Learned...

What Do I Look Forward To Tomorrow?

I Am Worthy Of:

Tatiana's Personal Note: Broken hearts do not last forever.

MORNING THOUGHTS

Date:

Mood:

Woke Up Feeling:

Today I Will Work On Thinking About?

What Do I Need Help With Today:

Today I Want God To Know:

Today I Affirm:

Today I Feel Tempted To:

Today's Break Up Symptoms:

The Reason Why I Will Not Do These Things
Even If My Mind Tries To Rationalize it
(Refer To Today I Feel Tempted To Question):

What Am I Doing Today To Make Me Happy?

What I Wish To Say To My Ex Today:

100

NIGHTLY THOUGHTS

How Do I Currently Feel? Why?

Do I Feel Better Than Yesterday?

Did My Ex Try To Get My Attention By Communicating With Me Or Anyone I Know In Any Way?

What Song Best Describes My Mood?

Did I Do A Good Job Protecting My Space Today?

I Am Thankful For?

What Could I Have Done A Better Job At Today?

Today I Learned...

What Do I Look Forward To Tomorrow?

I Am Worthy Of:

Tatiana's Personal Note: The break up was a set up for a breakthrough.

MORNING THOUGHTS

Date:

Mood:

Woke Up Feeling:

Today I Will Work On Thinking About?

What Do I Need Help With Today:

Today I Want God To Know:

Today I Affirm:

Today I Feel Tempted To:

Today's Break Up Symptoms:

The Reason Why I Will Not Do These Things Even If My Mind Tries To Rationalize it (Refer To Today I Feel Tempted To Question):

What Am I Doing Today To Make Me Happy?

What I Wish To Say To My Ex Today:

NIGHTLY THOUGHTS

How Do I Currently Feel? Why?

Do I Feel Better Than Yesterday?

Did My Ex Try To Get My Attention By Communicating With Me Or Anyone I Know In Any Way?

What Song Best Describes My Mood?

Did I Do A Good Job Protecting My Space Today?

I Am Thankful For?

What Could I Have Done A Better Job At Today?

Today I Learned...

What Do I Look Forward To Tomorrow?

I Am Worthy Of:

Tatiana's Personal Note: Sometimes the person who you think deserves you doesn't.

GOD IS GETTING YOU THROUGH IT

SHE LET GO OF WHAT COULD NOT PRESERVE HER AND REPLACED IT WITH WHAT FORTIFIED HER

MORNING THOUGHTS

Date:

Mood:

Woke Up Feeling:

Today I Will Work On Thinking About?

What Do I Need Help With Today:

Today I Want God To Know:

Today I Affirm:

Today I Feel Tempted To:

Today's Break Up Symptoms:

The Reason Why I Will Not Do These Things Even If My Mind Tries To Rationalize it (Refer To Today I Feel Tempted To Question):

What Am I Doing Today To Make Me Happy?

What I Wish To Say To My Ex Today:

NIGHTLY THOUGHTS

How Do I Currently Feel? Why?

Do I Feel Better Than Yesterday?

Did My Ex Try To Get My Attention By Communicating With Me Or Anyone I Know In Any Way?

What Song Best Describes My Mood?

Did I Do A Good Job Protecting My Space Today?

I Am Thankful For?

What Could I Have Done A Better Job At Today?

Today I Learned...

What Do I Look Forward To Tomorrow?

I Am Worthy Of:

Tatiana's Personal Note: What has gone is not better than what is coming.

MORNING THOUGHTS

Date:

Woke Up Feeling:

What Do I Need Help With Today:

Today I Affirm:

Today's Break Up Symptoms:

What Am I Doing Today To Make Me Happy?

Mood:

Today I Will Work On Thinking About?

Today I Want God To Know:

Today I Feel Tempted To:

The Reason Why I Will Not Do These Things Even If My Mind Tries To Rationalize it (Refer To Today I Feel Tempted To Question):

What I Wish To Say To My Ex Today:

NIGHTLY THOUGHTS

How Do I Currently Feel? Why?

Did My Ex Try To Get My Attention By Communicating With Me Or Anyone I Know In Any Way?

Did I Do A Good Job Protecting My Space Today?

What Could I Have Done A Better Job At Today?

What Do I Look Forward To Tomorrow?

Do I Feel Better Than Yesterday?

What Song Best Describes My Mood?

I Am Thankful For?

Today I Learned...

I Am Worthy Of:

Tatiana's Personal Note: She believed so much that it came to life. So now they believe.

MORNING THOUGHTS

Date:

Mood:

Woke Up Feeling:

Today I Will Work On Thinking About?

What Do I Need Help With Today:

Today I Want God To Know:

Today I Affirm:

Today I Feel Tempted To:

Today's Break Up Symptoms:

The Reason Why I Will Not Do These Things
Even If My Mind Tries To Rationalize it
(Refer To Today I Feel Tempted To Question):

What Am I Doing Today To Make Me Happy?

What I Wish To Say To My Ex Today:

NIGHTLY THOUGHTS

How Do I Currently Feel? Why?

Do I Feel Better Than Yesterday?

Did My Ex Try To Get My Attention By Communicating With Me Or Anyone I Know In Any Way?

What Song Best Describes My Mood?

Did I Do A Good Job Protecting My Space Today?

I Am Thankful For?

What Could I Have Done A Better Job At Today?

Today I Learned...

What Do I Look Forward To Tomorrow?

I Am Worthy Of:

Tatiana's Personal Note: True strength is knowing when to walk away from nonsense.

MORNING THOUGHTS

Date:

Mood:

Woke Up Feeling:

Today I Will Work On Thinking About?

What Do I Need Help With Today:

Today I Want God To Know:

Today I Affirm:

Today I Feel Tempted To:

Today's Break Up Symptoms:

The Reason Why I Will Not Do These Things Even If My Mind Tries To Rationalize it (Refer To Today I Feel Tempted To Question):

What Am I Doing Today To Make Me Happy?

What I Wish To Say To My Ex Today:

NIGHTLY THOUGHTS

How Do I Currently Feel? Why?

Do I Feel Better Than Yesterday?

Did My Ex Try To Get My Attention By Communicating With Me Or Anyone I Know In Any Way?

What Song Best Describes My Mood?

Did I Do A Good Job Protecting My Space Today?

I Am Thankful For?

What Could I Have Done A Better Job At Today?

Today I Learned...

What Do I Look Forward To Tomorrow?

I Am Worthy Of:

Tatiana's Personal Note: You are not just standing up for yourself. You are standing up for all those who are watching you.

MORNING THOUGHTS

Date: Mood:

Woke Up Feeling: Today I Will Work On Thinking About?

What Do I Need Help With Today: Today I Want God To Know:

Today I Affirm: Today I Feel Tempted To:

Today's Break Up Symptoms: The Reason Why I Will Not Do These Things
                                         Even If My Mind Tries To Rationalize it
                                         (Refer To Today I Feel Tempted To Question):

What Am I Doing Today To Make Me Happy?   What I Wish To Say To My Ex Today:

NIGHTLY THOUGHTS

How Do I Currently Feel? Why?

Do I Feel Better Than Yesterday?

Did My Ex Try To Get My Attention By Communicating With Me Or Anyone I Know In Any Way?

What Song Best Describes My Mood?

Did I Do A Good Job Protecting My Space Today?

I Am Thankful For?

What Could I Have Done A Better Job At Today?

Today I Learned...

What Do I Look Forward To Tomorrow?

I Am Worthy Of:

Tatiana's Personal Note: You are everything to somebody.

MY LIFE CHANGED WHEN I DECIDED TO BE HAPPY.... AGAIN.

NO MORE UNHEALTHY ATTACHMENTS

MORNING THOUGHTS

Date:

Mood:

Woke Up Feeling:

Today I Will Work On Thinking About?

What Do I Need Help With Today:

Today I Want God To Know:

Today I Affirm:

Today I Feel Tempted To:

Today's Break Up Symptoms:

The Reason Why I Will Not Do These Things
Even If My Mind Tries To Rationalize it
(Refer To Today I Feel Tempted To Question):

What Am I Doing Today To Make Me Happy?

What I Wish To Say To My Ex Today:

NIGHTLY THOUGHTS

How Do I Currently Feel? Why?

Do I Feel Better Than Yesterday?

Did My Ex Try To Get My Attention By Communicating With Me Or Anyone I Know In Any Way?

What Song Best Describes My Mood?

Did I Do A Good Job Protecting My Space Today?

I Am Thankful For?

What Could I Have Done A Better Job At Today?

Today I Learned...

What Do I Look Forward To Tomorrow?

I Am Worthy Of:

Tatiana's Personal Note: Let love guide your life. Not hurt.

MORNING THOUGHTS

Date:

Mood:

Woke Up Feeling:

Today I Will Work On Thinking About?

What Do I Need Help With Today:

Today I Want God To Know:

Today I Affirm:

Today I Feel Tempted To:

Today's Break Up Symptoms:

The Reason Why I Will Not Do These Things
Even If My Mind Tries To Rationalize it
(Refer To Today I Feel Tempted To Question):

What Am I Doing Today To Make Me Happy?

What I Wish To Say To My Ex Today:

NIGHTLY THOUGHTS

How Do I Currently Feel? Why?

Do I Feel Better Than Yesterday?

Did My Ex Try To Get My Attention By Communicating With Me Or Anyone I Know In Any Way?

What Song Best Describes My Mood?

Did I Do A Good Job Protecting My Space Today?

I Am Thankful For?

What Could I Have Done A Better Job At Today?

Today I Learned...

What Do I Look Forward To Tomorrow?

I Am Worthy Of:

Tatiana's Personal Note: Always believe in you.

MORNING THOUGHTS

Date:

Woke Up Feeling:

What Do I Need Help With Today:

Today I Affirm:

Today's Break Up Symptoms:

What Am I Doing Today To Make Me Happy?

Mood:

Today I Will Work On Thinking About?

Today I Want God To Know:

Today I Feel Tempted To:

The Reason Why I Will Not Do These Things Even If My Mind Tries To Rationalize it (Refer To Today I Feel Tempted To Question):

What I Wish To Say To My Ex Today:

NIGHTLY THOUGHTS

How Do I Currently Feel? Why?

Do I Feel Better Than Yesterday?

Did My Ex Try To Get My Attention By Communicating With Me Or Anyone I Know In Any Way?

What Song Best Describes My Mood?

Did I Do A Good Job Protecting My Space Today?

I Am Thankful For?

What Could I Have Done A Better Job At Today?

Today I Learned...

What Do I Look Forward To Tomorrow?

I Am Worthy Of:

Tatiana's Personal Note: Remember that the ones who criticize you are not perfect.

MORNING THOUGHTS

Date:

Mood:

Woke Up Feeling:

Today I Will Work On Thinking About?

What Do I Need Help With Today:

Today I Want God To Know:

Today I Affirm:

Today I Feel Tempted To:

Today's Break Up Symptoms:

The Reason Why I Will Not Do These Things Even If My Mind Tries To Rationalize it (Refer To Today I Feel Tempted To Question):

What Am I Doing Today To Make Me Happy?

What I Wish To Say To My Ex Today:

NIGHTLY THOUGHTS

How Do I Currently Feel? Why?

Did My Ex Try To Get My Attention By Communicating With Me Or Anyone I Know In Any Way?

Did I Do A Good Job Protecting My Space Today?

What Could I Have Done A Better Job At Today?

What Do I Look Forward To Tomorrow?

Do I Feel Better Than Yesterday?

What Song Best Describes My Mood?

I Am Thankful For?

Today I Learned...

I Am Worthy Of:

Tatiana's Personal Note: You must heal yourself first before you can truly win.

MORNING THOUGHTS

Date:

Mood:

Woke Up Feeling:

Today I Will Work On Thinking About?

What Do I Need Help With Today:

Today I Want God To Know:

Today I Affirm:

Today I Feel Tempted To:

Today's Break Up Symptoms:

The Reason Why I Will Not Do These Things Even If My Mind Tries To Rationalize it (Refer To Today I Feel Tempted To Question):

What Am I Doing Today To Make Me Happy?

What I Wish To Say To My Ex Today:

NIGHTLY THOUGHTS

How Do I Currently Feel? Why?

Did My Ex Try To Get My Attention By Communicating With Me Or Anyone I Know In Any Way?

Did I Do A Good Job Protecting My Space Today?

What Could I Have Done A Better Job At Today?

What Do I Look Forward To Tomorrow?

Do I Feel Better Than Yesterday?

What Song Best Describes My Mood?

I Am Thankful For?

Today I Learned...

I Am Worthy Of:

Tatiana's Personal Note: Your future does not have to look like your past.

YOU DO NOT UNDERSTAND WHAT I AM DOING NOW BUT SOMEDAY YOU WILL
-GOD

MORNING THOUGHTS

Date:

Woke Up Feeling:

What Do I Need Help With Today:

Today I Affirm:

Today's Break Up Symptoms:

What Am I Doing Today To Make Me Happy?

Mood:

Today I Will Work On Thinking About?

Today I Want God To Know:

Today I Feel Tempted To:

The Reason Why I Will Not Do These Things
Even If My Mind Tries To Rationalize it
(Refer To Today I Feel Tempted To Question):

What I Wish To Say To My Ex Today:

NIGHTLY THOUGHTS

How Do I Currently Feel? Why?

Do I Feel Better Than Yesterday?

Did My Ex Try To Get My Attention By Communicating With Me Or Anyone I Know In Any Way?

What Song Best Describes My Mood?

Did I Do A Good Job Protecting My Space Today?

I Am Thankful For?

What Could I Have Done A Better Job At Today?

Today I Learned...

What Do I Look Forward To Tomorrow?

I Am Worthy Of:

Tatiana's Personal Note: You don't have to pretend it doesn't hurt. You just have to leave what hurts you alone.

MORNING THOUGHTS

Date:

Mood:

Woke Up Feeling:

Today I Will Work On Thinking About?

What Do I Need Help With Today:

Today I Want God To Know:

Today I Affirm:

Today I Feel Tempted To:

Today's Break Up Symptoms:

The Reason Why I Will Not Do These Things Even If My Mind Tries To Rationalize it (Refer To Today I Feel Tempted To Question):

What Am I Doing Today To Make Me Happy?

What I Wish To Say To My Ex Today:

NIGHTLY THOUGHTS

How Do I Currently Feel? Why?

Do I Feel Better Than Yesterday?

Did My Ex Try To Get My Attention By Communicating With Me Or Anyone I Know In Any Way?

What Song Best Describes My Mood?

Did I Do A Good Job Protecting My Space Today?

I Am Thankful For?

What Could I Have Done A Better Job At Today?

Today I Learned...

What Do I Look Forward To Tomorrow?

I Am Worthy Of:

Tatiana's Personal Note: Your next blessing can show up at anytime.

MORNING THOUGHTS

Date:

Woke Up Feeling:

What Do I Need Help With Today:

Today I Affirm:

Today's Break Up Symptoms:

What Am I Doing Today To Make Me Happy?

Mood:

Today I Will Work On Thinking About?

Today I Want God To Know:

Today I Feel Tempted To:

The Reason Why I Will Not Do These Things
Even If My Mind Tries To Rationalize it
(Refer To Today I Feel Tempted To Question):

What I Wish To Say To My Ex Today:

NIGHTLY THOUGHTS

How Do I Currently Feel? Why?

Do I Feel Better Than Yesterday?

Did My Ex Try To Get My Attention By Communicating With Me Or Anyone I Know In Any Way?

What Song Best Describes My Mood?

Did I Do A Good Job Protecting My Space Today?

I Am Thankful For?

What Could I Have Done A Better Job At Today?

Today I Learned...

What Do I Look Forward To Tomorrow?

I Am Worthy Of:

Tatiana's Personal Note: Prepare for the woman you want to be.

I'VE GOT THIS

I AM MY BIGGEST PRIORITY

MORNING THOUGHTS

Date:

Woke Up Feeling:

What Do I Need Help With Today:

Today I Affirm:

Today's Break Up Symptoms:

What Am I Doing Today To Make Me Happy?

Mood:

Today I Will Work On Thinking About?

Today I Want God To Know:

Today I Feel Tempted To:

The Reason Why I Will Not Do These Things
Even If My Mind Tries To Rationalize it
(Refer To Today I Feel Tempted To Question):

What I Wish To Say To My Ex Today:

NIGHTLY THOUGHTS

How Do I Currently Feel? Why?

Do I Feel Better Than Yesterday?

Did My Ex Try To Get My Attention By Communicating With Me Or Anyone I Know In Any Way?

What Song Best Describes My Mood?

Did I Do A Good Job Protecting My Space Today?

I Am Thankful For?

What Could I Have Done A Better Job At Today?

Today I Learned...

What Do I Look Forward To Tomorrow?

I Am Worthy Of:

Tatiana's Personal Note: Don't know what to ask God for? Pray about that.

MORNING THOUGHTS

Date:

Mood:

Woke Up Feeling:

Today I Will Work On Thinking About?

What Do I Need Help With Today:

Today I Want God To Know:

Today I Affirm:

Today I Feel Tempted To:

Today's Break Up Symptoms:

The Reason Why I Will Not Do These Things
Even If My Mind Tries To Rationalize it
(Refer To Today I Feel Tempted To Question):

What Am I Doing Today To Make Me Happy?

What I Wish To Say To My Ex Today:

NIGHTLY THOUGHTS

How Do I Currently Feel? Why?

Do I Feel Better Than Yesterday?

Did My Ex Try To Get My Attention By Communicating With Me Or Anyone I Know In Any Way?

What Song Best Describes My Mood?

Did I Do A Good Job Protecting My Space Today?

I Am Thankful For?

What Could I Have Done A Better Job At Today?

Today I Learned...

What Do I Look Forward To Tomorrow?

I Am Worthy Of:

Tatiana's Personal Note: Just because it did not work out does not mean there is something wrong with you.

MORNING THOUGHTS

Date:

Mood:

Woke Up Feeling:

Today I Will Work On Thinking About?

What Do I Need Help With Today:

Today I Want God To Know:

Today I Affirm:

Today I Feel Tempted To:

Today's Break Up Symptoms:

The Reason Why I Will Not Do These Things
Even If My Mind Tries To Rationalize it
(Refer To Today I Feel Tempted To Question):

What Am I Doing Today To Make Me Happy?

What I Wish To Say To My Ex Today:

NIGHTLY THOUGHTS

How Do I Currently Feel? Why?

Do I Feel Better Than Yesterday?

Did My Ex Try To Get My Attention By Communicating With Me Or Anyone I Know In Any Way?

What Song Best Describes My Mood?

Did I Do A Good Job Protecting My Space Today?

I Am Thankful For?

What Could I Have Done A Better Job At Today?

Today I Learned...

What Do I Look Forward To Tomorrow?

I Am Worthy Of:

Tatiana's Personal Note: Always speak great things about you. Your spirit is listening.

MORNING THOUGHTS

Date:

Woke Up Feeling:

What Do I Need Help With Today:

Today I Affirm:

Today's Break Up Symptoms:

What Am I Doing Today To Make Me Happy?

Mood:

Today I Will Work On Thinking About?

Today I Want God To Know:

Today I Feel Tempted To:

The Reason Why I Will Not Do These Things
Even If My Mind Tries To Rationalize it
(Refer To Today I Feel Tempted To Question):

What I Wish To Say To My Ex Today:

NIGHTLY THOUGHTS

How Do I Currently Feel? Why?

Do I Feel Better Than Yesterday?

Did My Ex Try To Get My Attention By Communicating With Me Or Anyone I Know In Any Way?

What Song Best Describes My Mood?

Did I Do A Good Job Protecting My Space Today?

I Am Thankful For?

What Could I Have Done A Better Job At Today?

Today I Learned...

What Do I Look Forward To Tomorrow?

I Am Worthy Of:

Tatiana's Personal Note: Please remember that pain does not last forever.

OPINIONS, FEELINGS AND PRESENCE MATTER.

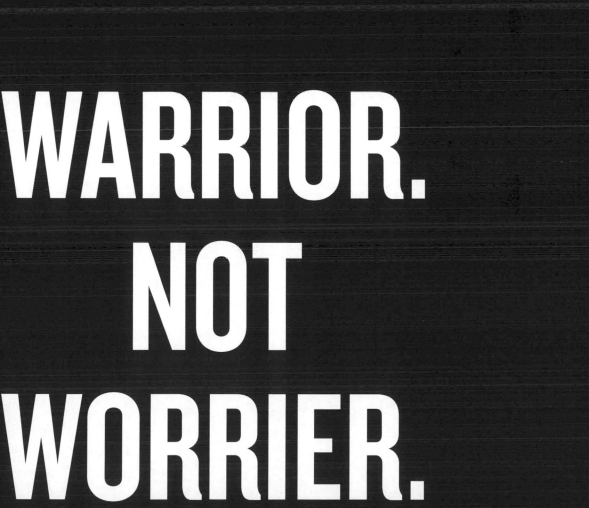

MORNING THOUGHTS

Date:

Mood:

Woke Up Feeling:

Today I Will Work On Thinking About?

What Do I Need Help With Today:

Today I Want God To Know:

Today I Affirm:

Today I Feel Tempted To:

Today's Break Up Symptoms:

The Reason Why I Will Not Do These Things
Even If My Mind Tries To Rationalize it
(Refer To Today I Feel Tempted To Question):

What Am I Doing Today To Make Me Happy?

What I Wish To Say To My Ex Today:

NIGHTLY THOUGHTS

How Do I Currently Feel? Why?

Do I Feel Better Than Yesterday?

Did My Ex Try To Get My Attention By Communicating With Me Or Anyone I Know In Any Way?

What Song Best Describes My Mood?

Did I Do A Good Job Protecting My Space Today?

I Am Thankful For?

What Could I Have Done A Better Job At Today?

Today I Learned...

What Do I Look Forward To Tomorrow?

I Am Worthy Of:

Tatiana's Personal Note: To someone who loves, you are everything they hoped for.

MORNING THOUGHTS

Date: Mood:

Woke Up Feeling: Today I Will Work On Thinking About?

What Do I Need Help With Today: Today I Want God To Know:

Today I Affirm: Today I Feel Tempted To:

Today's Break Up Symptoms: The Reason Why I Will Not Do These Things
                                              Even If My Mind Tries To Rationalize it
                                              (Refer To Today I Feel Tempted To Question):

What Am I Doing Today To Make Me Happy?   What I Wish To Say To My Ex Today:

NIGHTLY THOUGHTS

How Do I Currently Feel? Why?

Do I Feel Better Than Yesterday?

Did My Ex Try To Get My Attention By Communicating With Me Or Anyone I Know In Any Way?

What Song Best Describes My Mood?

Did I Do A Good Job Protecting My Space Today?

I Am Thankful For?

What Could I Have Done A Better Job At Today?

Today I Learned...

What Do I Look Forward To Tomorrow?

I Am Worthy Of:

Tatiana's Personal Note: If nothing else, at least you are a 'real one.'

MORNING THOUGHTS

Date:

Mood:

Woke Up Feeling:

Today I Will Work On Thinking About?

What Do I Need Help With Today:

Today I Want God To Know:

Today I Affirm:

Today I Feel Tempted To:

Today's Break Up Symptoms:

The Reason Why I Will Not Do These Things
Even If My Mind Tries To Rationalize it
(Refer To Today I Feel Tempted To Question):

What Am I Doing Today To Make Me Happy?

What I Wish To Say To My Ex Today:

NIGHTLY THOUGHTS

How Do I Currently Feel? Why?

Do I Feel Better Than Yesterday?

Did My Ex Try To Get My Attention By Communicating With Me Or Anyone I Know In Any Way?

What Song Best Describes My Mood?

Did I Do A Good Job Protecting My Space Today?

I Am Thankful For?

What Could I Have Done A Better Job At Today?

Today I Learned...

What Do I Look Forward To Tomorrow?

I Am Worthy Of:

Tatiana's Personal Note: At some point you realize you need you.

153

MORNING THOUGHTS

Date:

Mood:

Woke Up Feeling:

Today I Will Work On Thinking About?

What Do I Need Help With Today:

Today I Want God To Know:

Today I Affirm:

Today I Feel Tempted To:

Today's Break Up Symptoms:

The Reason Why I Will Not Do These Things
Even If My Mind Tries To Rationalize it
(Refer To Today I Feel Tempted To Question):

What Am I Doing Today To Make Me Happy?

What I Wish To Say To My Ex Today:

NIGHTLY THOUGHTS

How Do I Currently Feel? Why?

Do I Feel Better Than Yesterday?

Did My Ex Try To Get My Attention By Communicating With Me Or Anyone I Know In Any Way?

What Song Best Describes My Mood?

Did I Do A Good Job Protecting My Space Today?

I Am Thankful For?

What Could I Have Done A Better Job At Today?

Today I Learned...

What Do I Look Forward To Tomorrow?

I Am Worthy Of:

Tatiana's Personal Note: Sometimes you do not need closure. Sometimes you just need to move on.

MORNING THOUGHTS

Date:

Woke Up Feeling:

What Do I Need Help With Today:

Today I Affirm:

Today's Break Up Symptoms:

What Am I Doing Today To Make Me Happy?

Mood:

Today I Will Work On Thinking About?

Today I Want God To Know:

Today I Feel Tempted To:

The Reason Why I Will Not Do These Things
Even If My Mind Tries To Rationalize it
(Refer To Today I Feel Tempted To Question):

What I Wish To Say To My Ex Today:

NIGHTLY THOUGHTS

How Do I Currently Feel? Why?

Do I Feel Better Than Yesterday?

Did My Ex Try To Get My Attention By Communicating With Me Or Anyone I Know In Any Way?

What Song Best Describes My Mood?

Did I Do A Good Job Protecting My Space Today?

I Am Thankful For?

What Could I Have Done A Better Job At Today?

Today I Learned...

What Do I Look Forward To Tomorrow?

I Am Worthy Of:

Tatiana's Personal Note: Somethings are temporary but the love you have for yourself should be forever.

MORNING THOUGHTS

Date: Mood:

Woke Up Feeling: Today I Will Work On Thinking About?

What Do I Need Help With Today: Today I Want God To Know:

Today I Affirm: Today I Feel Tempted To:

Today's Break Up Symptoms: The Reason Why I Will Not Do These Things
                                               Even If My Mind Tries To Rationalize it
                                               (Refer To Today I Feel Tempted To Question):

What Am I Doing Today To Make Me Happy?   What I Wish To Say To My Ex Today:

NIGHTLY THOUGHTS

How Do I Currently Feel? Why?

Did My Ex Try To Get My Attention By Communicating With Me Or Anyone I Know In Any Way?

Did I Do A Good Job Protecting My Space Today?

What Could I Have Done A Better Job At Today?

What Do I Look Forward To Tomorrow?

Do I Feel Better Than Yesterday?

What Song Best Describes My Mood?

I Am Thankful For?

Today I Learned...

I Am Worthy Of:

Tatiana's Personal Note: I use my pain to empower me not control me. I turned my pain into my motivation.

OWN WHO YOU ARE.

I WANT WHAT GOD WANTS FOR ME.

MORNING THOUGHTS

Date: Mood:

Woke Up Feeling: Today I Will Work On Thinking About?

What Do I Need Help With Today: Today I Want God To Know:

Today I Affirm: Today I Feel Tempted To:

Today's Break Up Symptoms: The Reason Why I Will Not Do These Things
                                                Even If My Mind Tries To Rationalize it
                                                (Refer To Today I Feel Tempted To Question):

What Am I Doing Today To Make Me Happy?   What I Wish To Say To My Ex Today:

NIGHTLY THOUGHTS

How Do I Currently Feel? Why?

Do I Feel Better Than Yesterday?

Did My Ex Try To Get My Attention By Communicating With Me Or Anyone I Know In Any Way?

What Song Best Describes My Mood?

Did I Do A Good Job Protecting My Space Today?

I Am Thankful For?

What Could I Have Done A Better Job At Today?

Today I Learned...

What Do I Look Forward To Tomorrow?

I Am Worthy Of:

Tatiana's Personal Note: It does not matter what they see. It just matters what you see.

SECTION 2: ITS BEEN AWHILE BUT NOW I'M BACK

ABOUT THIS SECTION

You have now moved into the section where the focus is on you. This means you are about to explore what it truly means to attend to your needs. You will be examining what you are letting go of as well as develop a full understanding of what habits and thoughts you are picking up to make yourself stronger. It's in this section you will evaluate if you truly understand who you are becoming. You will realize that no one's words can affect you unless you allow it. As of right now, how you view yourself and what you think about yourself is what matters the most. You will learn how to nurture yourself from within and begin to view your thoughts, your peace and your time as valuable.

I recommend filling out these questions during your morning routine. This will set the tone for your day and keep you focused on your personal goals. Let's get started.

Date:	Mood:
Define Yourself Today:	What I Thought I Had In My Previous Relationship But Have Found In Me?
Today I Affirm:	What I Want God To Know:
Today I Set Myself Free From:	Today I Nurtured Myself By:
Today's Desire:	Today's New Thought:
What I Lost In My Previous Relationship But Have Regained Today?	The New Thing I Tried Today:

Tatiana's Personal Note: When someone tells you that you are beautiful. . .believe them. That is God admiring his work.

Date:	Mood:
Define Yourself Today:	What I Thought I Had In My Previous Relationship But Have Found In Me?
Today I Affirm:	What I Want God To Know:
Today I Set Myself Free From:	Today I Nurtured Myself By:
Today's Desire:	Today's New Thought:
What I Lost In My Previous Relationship But Have Regained Today?	The New Thing I Tried Today:

Tatiana's Personal Note: A great life is built on loving God, yourself and others.

Date:

Mood:

Define Yourself Today:

What I Thought I Had In My Previous Relationship But Have Found In Me?

Today I Affirm:

What I Want God To Know:

Today I Set Myself Free From:

Today I Nurtured Myself By:

Today's Desire:

Today's New Thought:

What I Lost In My Previous Relationship But Have Regained Today?

The New Thing I Tried Today:

Tatiana's Personal Note: Learn to live in peace.

Date:

Mood:

Define Yourself Today:

What I Thought I Had In My Previous Relationship But Have Found In Me?

Today I Affirm:

What I Want God To Know:

Today I Set Myself Free From:

Today I Nurtured Myself By:

Today's Desire:

Today's New Thought:

What I Lost In My Previous Relationship But Have Regained Today?

The New Thing I Tried Today:

Tatiana's Personal Note: First be a great friend to you.

Date: Mood:

Define Yourself Today: What I Thought I Had In My Previous
                                         Relationship But Have Found In Me?

Today I Affirm: What I Want God To Know:

Today I Set Myself Free From: Today I Nurtured Myself By:

Today's Desire: Today's New Thought:

What I Lost In My Previous Relationship The New Thing I Tried Today:
But Have Regained Today?

Tatiana's Personal Note: Take care of your soul.

Date:	Mood:
Define Yourself Today:	What I Thought I Had In My Previous Relationship But Have Found In Me?
Today I Affirm:	What I Want God To Know:
Today I Set Myself Free From:	Today I Nurtured Myself By:
Today's Desire:	Today's New Thought:
What I Lost In My Previous Relationship But Have Regained Today?	The New Thing I Tried Today:

Tatiana's Personal Note: They will always wonder how you win.

I'M NOT AFRAID OF MY LOVE

NOTHING CAN STOP MY GLOW

Date: Mood:

Define Yourself Today: What I Thought I Had In My Previous
                                         Relationship But Have Found In Me?

Today I Affirm: What I Want God To Know:

Today I Set Myself Free From: Today I Nurtured Myself By:

Today's Desire: Today's New Thought:

What I Lost In My Previous Relationship The New Thing I Tried Today:
But Have Regained Today?

Tatiana's Personal Note: Good hearts do exist.

Date:	Mood:
Define Yourself Today:	What I Thought I Had In My Previous Relationship But Have Found In Me?
Today I Affirm:	What I Want God To Know:
Today I Set Myself Free From:	Today I Nurtured Myself By:
Today's Desire:	Today's New Thought:
What I Lost In My Previous Relationship But Have Regained Today?	The New Thing I Tried Today:

Tatiana's Personal Note: Grow and fall in love.

Date:

Define Yourself Today:

Today I Affirm:

Today I Set Myself Free From:

Today's Desire:

What I Lost In My Previous Relationship But Have Regained Today?

Mood:

What I Thought I Had In My Previous Relationship But Have Found In Me?

What I Want God To Know:

Today I Nurtured Myself By:

Today's New Thought:

The New Thing I Tried Today:

Tatiana's Personal Note: You are what someone is dreaming about.

Date: Mood:

Define Yourself Today: What I Thought I Had In My Previous
                                         Relationship But Have Found In Me?

Today I Affirm: What I Want God To Know:

Today I Set Myself Free From: Today I Nurtured Myself By:

Today's Desire: Today's New Thought:

What I Lost In My Previous Relationship The New Thing I Tried Today:
But Have Regained Today?

Tatiana's Personal Note: Always be the first to choose you.

I HAVE LEARNED NOTHING I WENT THROUGH WAS A WASTE OF TIME. DO YOU NOT SEE HOW MY STORY IS UNFOLDING? PAY ATTENTION.

I CAN NOW LAUGH AT WHAT I THOUGHT I WANTED

Date:

Define Yourself Today:

Today I Affirm:

Today I Set Myself Free From:

Today's Desire:

What I Lost In My Previous Relationship But Have Regained Today?

Mood:

What I Thought I Had In My Previous Relationship But Have Found In Me?

What I Want God To Know:

Today I Nurtured Myself By:

Today's New Thought:

The New Thing I Tried Today:

Tatiana's Personal Note: Always remember you were built for greatness.

Date:

Define Yourself Today:

Today I Affirm:

Today I Set Myself Free From:

Today's Desire:

What I Lost In My Previous Relationship
But Have Regained Today?

Mood:

What I Thought I Had In My Previous
Relationship But Have Found In Me?

What I Want God To Know:

Today I Nurtured Myself By:

Today's New Thought:

The New Thing I Tried Today:

*Tatiana's Personal Note: What was supposed to harm you, embarrass you, destroy
you and play you did not know it was simply a blessing to you.*

Date: Mood:

Define Yourself Today: What I Thought I Had In My Previous
                                               Relationship But Have Found In Me?

Today I Affirm: What I Want God To Know:

Today I Set Myself Free From: Today I Nurtured Myself By:

Today's Desire: Today's New Thought:

What I Lost In My Previous Relationship   The New Thing I Tried Today:
But Have Regained Today?

Tatiana's Personal Note: It is not easy but it gets better.

Date:

Define Yourself Today:

Today I Affirm:

Today I Set Myself Free From:

Today's Desire:

What I Lost In My Previous Relationship But Have Regained Today?

Mood:

What I Thought I Had In My Previous Relationship But Have Found In Me?

What I Want God To Know:

Today I Nurtured Myself By:

Today's New Thought:

The New Thing I Tried Today:

Tatiana's Personal Note: Allow what wants to go to go, so that you can allow what needs to come to come.

YOU DO NOT NEED ANYONE'S VALIDATION. YOU'VE GOT THIS.

AS SOON AS I STARTED HEALING THE PARTS OF ME THAT WERE HURT, I STOPPED ATTRACTING BROKEN PEOPLE.

Date:

Define Yourself Today:

Today I Affirm:

Today I Set Myself Free From:

Today's Desire:

What I Lost In My Previous Relationship But Have Regained Today?

Mood:

What I Thought I Had In My Previous Relationship But Have Found In Me?

What I Want God To Know:

Today I Nurtured Myself By:

Today's New Thought:

The New Thing I Tried Today:

Tatiana's Personal Note: They may have been with you, but they were never for you.

Date: | Mood:

Define Yourself Today: | What I Thought I Had In My Previous Relationship But Have Found In Me?

Today I Affirm: | What I Want God To Know:

Today I Set Myself Free From: | Today I Nurtured Myself By:

Today's Desire: | Today's New Thought:

What I Lost In My Previous Relationship But Have Regained Today? | The New Thing I Tried Today:

Tatiana's Personal Note: You would never need to beg for something that you can give to yourself.

Date:

Define Yourself Today:

Today I Affirm:

Today I Set Myself Free From:

Today's Desire:

What I Lost In My Previous Relationship But Have Regained Today?

Mood:

What I Thought I Had In My Previous Relationship But Have Found In Me?

What I Want God To Know:

Today I Nurtured Myself By:

Today's New Thought:

The New Thing I Tried Today:

Tatiana's Personal Note: There is nothing wrong with over-loving yourself.

Date:

Define Yourself Today:

Today I Affirm:

Today I Set Myself Free From:

Today's Desire:

What I Lost In My Previous Relationship But Have Regained Today?

Mood:

What I Thought I Had In My Previous Relationship But Have Found In Me?

What I Want God To Know:

Today I Nurtured Myself By:

Today's New Thought:

The New Thing I Tried Today:

Tatiana's Personal Note: Being whole all by yourself …. that is more than enough.

Date:

Mood:

Define Yourself Today:

What I Thought I Had In My Previous Relationship But Have Found In Me?

Today I Affirm:

What I Want God To Know:

Today I Set Myself Free From:

Today I Nurtured Myself By:

Today's Desire:

Today's New Thought:

What I Lost In My Previous Relationship But Have Regained Today?

The New Thing I Tried Today:

Tatiana's Personal Note: Never be afraid to shine.

Date:

Define Yourself Today:

Today I Affirm:

Today I Set Myself Free From:

Today's Desire:

What I Lost In My Previous Relationship But Have Regained Today?

Mood:

What I Thought I Had In My Previous Relationship But Have Found In Me?

What I Want God To Know:

Today I Nurtured Myself By:

Today's New Thought:

The New Thing I Tried Today:

Tatiana's Personal Note: Be in the business of investing in yourself.

Date:

Define Yourself Today:

Today I Affirm:

Today I Set Myself Free From:

Today's Desire:

What I Lost In My Previous Relationship But Have Regained Today?

Mood:

What I Thought I Had In My Previous Relationship But Have Found In Me?

What I Want God To Know:

Today I Nurtured Myself By:

Today's New Thought:

The New Thing I Tried Today:

Tatiana's Personal Note: It is time to level up.

I WILL NOT ALWAYS FIT IN .... NOR AM I TRYING TO

YOU WERE MEANT TO SEE BEAUTIFUL THINGS IN HUMBLE PLACES WITHIN YOU

Date:

Define Yourself Today:

Today I Affirm:

Today I Set Myself Free From:

Today's Desire:

What I Lost In My Previous Relationship But Have Regained Today?

Mood:

What I Thought I Had In My Previous Relationship But Have Found In Me?

What I Want God To Know:

Today I Nurtured Myself By:

Today's New Thought:

The New Thing I Tried Today:

Tatiana's Personal Note: Release. Replenish. Revamp.

Date:

Define Yourself Today:

Today I Affirm:

Today I Set Myself Free From:

Today's Desire:

What I Lost In My Previous Relationship But Have Regained Today?

Mood:

What I Thought I Had In My Previous Relationship But Have Found In Me?

What I Want God To Know:

Today I Nurtured Myself By:

Today's New Thought:

The New Thing I Tried Today:

Tatiana's Personal Note: Always stay grateful.

Date: Mood:

Define Yourself Today: What I Thought I Had In My Previous
                                               Relationship But Have Found In Me?

Today I Affirm: What I Want God To Know:

Today I Set Myself Free From: Today I Nurtured Myself By:

Today's Desire: Today's New Thought:

What I Lost In My Previous Relationship   The New Thing I Tried Today:
But Have Regained Today?

Tatiana's Personal Note: You do not need anyone's permission to shine.

Date:

Define Yourself Today:

Today I Affirm:

Today I Set Myself Free From:

Today's Desire:

What I Lost In My Previous Relationship But Have Regained Today?

Mood:

What I Thought I Had In My Previous Relationship But Have Found In Me?

What I Want God To Know:

Today I Nurtured Myself By:

Today's New Thought:

The New Thing I Tried Today:

Tatiana's Personal Note: All of you needs you.

Date:

Define Yourself Today:

Today I Affirm:

Today I Set Myself Free From:

Today's Desire:

What I Lost In My Previous Relationship But Have Regained Today?

Mood:

What I Thought I Had In My Previous Relationship But Have Found In Me?

What I Want God To Know:

Today I Nurtured Myself By:

Today's New Thought:

The New Thing I Tried Today:

Tatiana's Personal Note: You deserve to give yourself the best version of you.

I AM SELECTIVE.
I'M OKAY WITH THAT.

I BELONG TO ME BEFORE I BELONG TO ANYONE ELSE.

Date:

Define Yourself Today:

Today I Affirm:

Today I Set Myself Free From:

Today's Desire:

What I Lost In My Previous Relationship But Have Regained Today?

Mood:

What I Thought I Had In My Previous Relationship But Have Found In Me?

What I Want God To Know:

Today I Nurtured Myself By:

Today's New Thought:

The New Thing I Tried Today:

Tatiana's Personal Note: Trust in God's process.

Date:

Mood:

Define Yourself Today:

What I Thought I Had In My Previous Relationship But Have Found In Me?

Today I Affirm:

What I Want God To Know:

Today I Set Myself Free From:

Today I Nurtured Myself By:

Today's Desire:

Today's New Thought:

What I Lost In My Previous Relationship But Have Regained Today?

The New Thing I Tried Today:

Tatiana's Personal Note: Learn to nurture you.

Date:

Define Yourself Today:

Today I Affirm:

Today I Set Myself Free From:

Today's Desire:

What I Lost In My Previous Relationship But Have Regained Today?

Mood:

What I Thought I Had In My Previous Relationship But Have Found In Me?

What I Want God To Know:

Today I Nurtured Myself By:

Today's New Thought:

The New Thing I Tried Today:

Tatiana's Personal Note: It is okay if your happiness is obnoxious to others. Get rid of the others.

Date:	Mood:
Define Yourself Today:	What I Thought I Had In My Previous Relationship But Have Found In Me?
Today I Affirm:	What I Want God To Know:
Today I Set Myself Free From:	Today I Nurtured Myself By:
Today's Desire:	Today's New Thought:
What I Lost In My Previous Relationship But Have Regained Today?	The New Thing I Tried Today:

Tatiana's Personal Note: God has answered your prayer.

Date: Mood:

Define Yourself Today: What I Thought I Had In My Previous
                                           Relationship But Have Found In Me?

Today I Affirm: What I Want God To Know:

Today I Set Myself Free From: Today I Nurtured Myself By:

Today's Desire: Today's New Thought:

What I Lost In My Previous Relationship   The New Thing I Tried Today:
But Have Regained Today?

Tatiana's Personal Note: Be prepared for joy.

Date:	Mood:
Define Yourself Today:	What I Thought I Had In My Previous Relationship But Have Found In Me?
Today I Affirm:	What I Want God To Know:
Today I Set Myself Free From:	Today I Nurtured Myself By:
Today's Desire:	Today's New Thought:
What I Lost In My Previous Relationship But Have Regained Today?	The New Thing I Tried Today:

Tatiana's Personal Note: Show up for yourself.

Date: Mood:

Define Yourself Today: What I Thought I Had In My Previous
                                               Relationship But Have Found In Me?

Today I Affirm: What I Want God To Know:

Today I Set Myself Free From: Today I Nurtured Myself By:

Today's Desire: Today's New Thought:

What I Lost In My Previous Relationship   The New Thing I Tried Today:
But Have Regained Today?

Tatiana's Personal Note: Receive love. Love yourself.

IT FEELS GOOD TO BE REMOVED FROM THE CHAOS

THEY WILL START TO MISS YOU WHEN YOU AR DOING GOOD

Date:

Define Yourself Today:

Today I Affirm:

Today I Set Myself Free From:

Today's Desire:

What I Lost In My Previous Relationship But Have Regained Today?

Mood:

What I Thought I Had In My Previous Relationship But Have Found In Me?

What I Want God To Know:

Today I Nurtured Myself By:

Today's New Thought:

The New Thing I Tried Today:

Tatiana's Personal Note: Forgiveness is love. Show love to yourself.

Date: Mood:

Define Yourself Today: What I Thought I Had In My Previous
                                         Relationship But Have Found In Me?

Today I Affirm: What I Want God To Know:

Today I Set Myself Free From: Today I Nurtured Myself By:

Today's Desire: Today's New Thought:

What I Lost In My Previous Relationship The New Thing I Tried Today:
But Have Regained Today?

Tatiana's Personal Note: They will never be able to tell your story like you can. That's okay.

Date: Mood:

Define Yourself Today: What I Thought I Had In My Previous
                                               Relationship But Have Found In Me?

Today I Affirm: What I Want God To Know:

Today I Set Myself Free From: Today I Nurtured Myself By:

Today's Desire: Today's New Thought:

What I Lost In My Previous Relationship   The New Thing I Tried Today:
But Have Regained Today?

Tatiana's Personal Note: Your values are nonnegotiable.

Date:

Define Yourself Today:

Today I Affirm:

Today I Set Myself Free From:

Today's Desire:

What I Lost In My Previous Relationship But Have Regained Today?

Mood:

What I Thought I Had In My Previous Relationship But Have Found In Me?

What I Want God To Know:

Today I Nurtured Myself By:

Today's New Thought:

The New Thing I Tried Today:

Tatiana's Personal Note: Another person's opinion of you will never matter.

Date:

Define Yourself Today:

Today I Affirm:

Today I Set Myself Free From:

Today's Desire:

What I Lost In My Previous Relationship But Have Regained Today?

Mood:

What I Thought I Had In My Previous Relationship But Have Found In Me?

What I Want God To Know:

Today I Nurtured Myself By:

Today's New Thought:

The New Thing I Tried Today:

Tatiana's Personal Note: Some great things are happening to you right now.

Date: Mood:

Define Yourself Today: What I Thought I Had In My Previous
                                                   Relationship But Have Found In Me?

Today I Affirm: What I Want God To Know:

Today I Set Myself Free From: Today I Nurtured Myself By:

Today's Desire: Today's New Thought:

What I Lost In My Previous Relationship   The New Thing I Tried Today:
But Have Regained Today?

Tatiana's Personal Note: It is okay to start over with a new set of standards.

Date: Mood:

Define Yourself Today: What I Thought I Had In My Previous
                                               Relationship But Have Found In Me?

Today I Affirm: What I Want God To Know:

Today I Set Myself Free From: Today I Nurtured Myself By:

Today's Desire: Today's New Thought:

What I Lost In My Previous Relationship   The New Thing I Tried Today:
But Have Regained Today?

Tatiana's Personal Note: Remember you are not what they are used to.

217

I LOST THEM SO THAT I WOULD NOT HURT ANYMORE.

MY VOICE
MATTERS

Date:	Mood:
Define Yourself Today:	What I Thought I Had In My Previous Relationship But Have Found In Me?
Today I Affirm:	What I Want God To Know:
Today I Set Myself Free From:	Today I Nurtured Myself By:
Today's Desire:	Today's New Thought:
What I Lost In My Previous Relationship But Have Regained Today?	The New Thing I Tried Today:

Tatiana's Personal Note: Sometimes they think if you lose them, you've lost in life. They didn't realize that you've actually won.

Date:

Define Yourself Today:

Today I Affirm:

Today I Set Myself Free From:

Today's Desire:

What I Lost In My Previous Relationship
But Have Regained Today?

Mood:

What I Thought I Had In My Previous
Relationship But Have Found In Me?

What I Want God To Know:

Today I Nurtured Myself By:

Today's New Thought:

The New Thing I Tried Today:

Tatiana's Personal Note: You need you to love you.

Date: Mood:

Define Yourself Today: What I Thought I Had In My Previous
                                         Relationship But Have Found In Me?

Today I Affirm: What I Want God To Know:

Today I Set Myself Free From: Today I Nurtured Myself By:

Today's Desire: Today's New Thought:

What I Lost In My Previous Relationship The New Thing I Tried Today:
But Have Regained Today?

Tatiana's Personal Note: The old way will never measure up to your new mindset.

PEACE OF MIND.

I WANT THAT.

MY SELF-CARE IS
NOT A SECRET.

Date:

Define Yourself Today:

Today I Affirm:

Today I Set Myself Free From:

Today's Desire:

What I Lost In My Previous Relationship But Have Regained Today?

Mood:

What I Thought I Had In My Previous Relationship But Have Found In Me?

What I Want God To Know:

Today I Nurtured Myself By:

Today's New Thought:

The New Thing I Tried Today:

Tatiana's Personal Note: You are worthy of true love.

Date:

Define Yourself Today:

Today I Affirm:

Today I Set Myself Free From:

Today's Desire:

What I Lost In My Previous Relationship But Have Regained Today?

Mood:

What I Thought I Had In My Previous Relationship But Have Found In Me?

What I Want God To Know:

Today I Nurtured Myself By:

Today's New Thought:

The New Thing I Tried Today:

Tatiana's Personal Note: No more thinking small towards the things you want in life.

Date:

Define Yourself Today:

Today I Affirm:

Today I Set Myself Free From:

Today's Desire:

What I Lost In My Previous Relationship But Have Regained Today?

Mood:

What I Thought I Had In My Previous Relationship But Have Found In Me?

What I Want God To Know:

Today I Nurtured Myself By:

Today's New Thought:

The New Thing I Tried Today:

Tatiana's Personal Note: Your future does not have to look like your past.

Date:

Define Yourself Today:

Today I Affirm:

Today I Set Myself Free From:

Today's Desire:

What I Lost In My Previous Relationship But Have Regained Today?

Mood:

What I Thought I Had In My Previous Relationship But Have Found In Me?

What I Want God To Know:

Today I Nurtured Myself By:

Today's New Thought:

The New Thing I Tried Today:

Tatiana's Personal Note: Declare your greatness today.

Date:

Define Yourself Today:

Today I Affirm:

Today I Set Myself Free From:

Today's Desire:

What I Lost In My Previous Relationship But Have Regained Today?

Mood:

What I Thought I Had In My Previous Relationship But Have Found In Me?

What I Want God To Know:

Today I Nurtured Myself By:

Today's New Thought:

The New Thing I Tried Today:

Tatiana's Personal Note: Your faith is your biggest blessing.

Date: Mood:

Define Yourself Today: What I Thought I Had In My Previous
                                                         Relationship But Have Found In Me?

Today I Affirm: What I Want God To Know:

Today I Set Myself Free From: Today I Nurtured Myself By:

Today's Desire: Today's New Thought:

What I Lost In My Previous Relationship   The New Thing I Tried Today:
But Have Regained Today?

Tatiana's Personal Note: You are more than your mistakes.

Date:	Mood:
Define Yourself Today:	What I Thought I Had In My Previous Relationship But Have Found In Me?
Today I Affirm:	What I Want God To Know:
Today I Set Myself Free From:	Today I Nurtured Myself By:
Today's Desire:	Today's New Thought:
What I Lost In My Previous Relationship But Have Regained Today?	The New Thing I Tried Today:

Tatiana's Personal Note: There is greatness within you.

I WILL ALWAYS BE THE FIRST TO CHOOSE ME

I WANT YOU TO FEEL EVERY BIT OF ME ... EVEN THE PARTS THAT HURT. MAYBE THEN YOU WILL UNDERSTAND.

Date: | Mood:

Define Yourself Today: | What I Thought I Had In My Previous Relationship But Have Found In Me?

Today I Affirm: | What I Want God To Know:

Today I Set Myself Free From: | Today I Nurtured Myself By:

Today's Desire: | Today's New Thought:

What I Lost In My Previous Relationship But Have Regained Today? | The New Thing I Tried Today:

Tatiana's Personal Note: You can choose to move on to the next level of you at any time.

Date: Mood:

Define Yourself Today: What I Thought I Had In My Previous
                                         Relationship But Have Found In Me?

Today I Affirm: What I Want God To Know:

Today I Set Myself Free From: Today I Nurtured Myself By:

Today's Desire: Today's New Thought:

What I Lost In My Previous Relationship The New Thing I Tried Today:
But Have Regained Today?

Tatiana's Personal Note: Promise yourself to always connect with good energy.

Date:

Define Yourself Today:

Today I Affirm:

Today I Set Myself Free From:

Today's Desire:

What I Lost In My Previous Relationship But Have Regained Today?

Mood:

What I Thought I Had In My Previous Relationship But Have Found In Me?

What I Want God To Know:

Today I Nurtured Myself By:

Today's New Thought:

The New Thing I Tried Today:

Tatiana's Personal Note: Give yourself the love you easily give to others.

Date:	Mood:
Define Yourself Today:	What I Thought I Had In My Previous Relationship But Have Found In Me?
Today I Affirm:	What I Want God To Know:
Today I Set Myself Free From:	Today I Nurtured Myself By:
Today's Desire:	Today's New Thought:
What I Lost In My Previous Relationship But Have Regained Today?	The New Thing I Tried Today:

Tatiana's Personal Note: You do not have to ride the wave when you are the wave.

I WILL NOT TRY TO WIN ANYBODY'S LOVE

I TOLD MYSELF .... I GOT YOU.

Date:

Define Yourself Today:

Mood:

What I Thought I Had In My Previous Relationship But Have Found In Me?

Today I Affirm:

What I Want God To Know:

Today I Set Myself Free From:

Today I Nurtured Myself By:

Today's Desire:

Today's New Thought:

What I Lost In My Previous Relationship But Have Regained Today?

The New Thing I Tried Today:

Tatiana's Personal Note: It's time to get your confidence at a full tank.

Date:	Mood:
Define Yourself Today:	What I Thought I Had In My Previous Relationship But Have Found In Me?
Today I Affirm:	What I Want God To Know:
Today I Set Myself Free From:	Today I Nurtured Myself By:
Today's Desire:	Today's New Thought:
What I Lost In My Previous Relationship But Have Regained Today?	The New Thing I Tried Today:

Tatiana's Personal Note: That someone special in your life is you.

Date:

Mood:

Define Yourself Today:

What I Thought I Had In My Previous Relationship But Have Found In Me?

Today I Affirm:

What I Want God To Know:

Today I Set Myself Free From:

Today I Nurtured Myself By:

Today's Desire:

Today's New Thought:

What I Lost In My Previous Relationship But Have Regained Today?

The New Thing I Tried Today:

Tatiana's Personal Note: No longer will the fears of your past prevent you from creating a better future.

Date:	Mood:
Define Yourself Today:	What I Thought I Had In My Previous Relationship But Have Found In Me?
Today I Affirm:	What I Want God To Know:
Today I Set Myself Free From:	Today I Nurtured Myself By:
Today's Desire:	Today's New Thought:
What I Lost In My Previous Relationship But Have Regained Today?	The New Thing I Tried Today:

Tatiana's Personal Note: Too many people settle. So glad you are not one of them.

Date: Mood:

Define Yourself Today: What I Thought I Had In My Previous
                                               Relationship But Have Found In Me?

Today I Affirm: What I Want God To Know:

Today I Set Myself Free From: Today I Nurtured Myself By:

Today's Desire: Today's New Thought:

What I Lost In My Previous Relationship   The New Thing I Tried Today:
But Have Regained Today?

Tatiana's Personal Note: The LORD is my strength and my defense; he has become my salvation. – Psalms 118:14

Date:	Mood:
Define Yourself Today:	What I Thought I Had In My Previous Relationship But Have Found In Me?
Today I Affirm:	What I Want God To Know:
Today I Set Myself Free From:	Today I Nurtured Myself By:
Today's Desire:	Today's New Thought:
What I Lost In My Previous Relationship But Have Regained Today?	The New Thing I Tried Today:

Tatana's Personal Note: You can feel when the love is real.

SECTION 3: TELL THEM WATCH IT. I AM NOT JUST ANYBODY.

ABOUT THIS SECTION

Welcome to freedom. You have left the old behind. This section is all about envisioning and expecting everything you want and deserve in your love life. You may have had previous thoughts that dismissed any invitation for a new relationship and love in general, but this section is designed to break down all walls that prevent you from receiving what is a commandment from God - Love. Why not create and believe for a new chance at love with a romantic partner? Whether you currently have a partner or not, you can still believe for a healthy, passionate, respectful and responsible love life.

Before you create and believe in love with a romantic partner, you must know where you stand with yourself. What kinds of promises do you want to make to yourself? What do you want God to know? How will you know that you have found the one? Do you understand what you want and need from your next relationship?

Answer these questions in the beginning of the day and spend some time elaborating on your response. Don't just write what you want. Know that what you want is something you believe in for yourself. If you do not believe it for yourself, make the extra effort to work on believing it can happen for you. Get excited and have fun. Watch what you write come true.

Date: Mood:

Today I Affirm: My Future Relationship Will Feel:

Today I Feel: Today I Ask God For:

Today's Intention: Today I Release _____
                                         And Hope To Gain

Today's Relationship With   I Am Excited About:

_____

Looks Like: I Promise Myself:

My Next Partner Will:

Tatiana's Personal Note: Remember that what tried to hurt you helped you.

248

Date:

Today I Affirm:

Today I Feel:

Today's Intention:

Today's Relationship With

_____

Looks Like:

My Next Partner Will:

Mood:

My Future Relationship Will Feel:

Today I Ask God For:

Today I Release _____
And Hope To Gain

I Am Excited About:

I Promise Myself:

Tatiana's Personal Note: Believe in the best for yourself.

Date:

Today I Affirm:

Today I Feel:

Today's Intention:

Today's Relationship With

_____

Looks Like:

My Next Partner Will:

Mood:

My Future Relationship Will Feel:

Today I Ask God For:

Today I Release _____
And Hope To Gain

I Am Excited About:

I Promise Myself:

Tatiana's Personal Note: Believe in yourself before anyone else can.

Date: Mood:

Today I Affirm: My Future Relationship Will Feel:

Today I Feel: Today I Ask God For:

Today's Intention: Today I Release _____
                                         And Hope To Gain

Today's Relationship With   I Am Excited About:

_____

Looks Like: I Promise Myself:

My Next Partner Will:

Tatiana's Personal Note: Don't be afraid to go after everything you've ever wanted.

Date: | Mood:

Today I Affirm: | My Future Relationship Will Feel:

Today I Feel: | Today I Ask God For:

Today's Intention: | Today I Release _____
And Hope To Gain

Today's Relationship With | I Am Excited About:

_____

Looks Like: | I Promise Myself:

My Next Partner Will:

Tatiana's Personal Note: Do not let your fear of being hurt make you miss the chance to be happy.

Date: Mood:

Today I Affirm: My Future Relationship Will Feel:

Today I Feel: Today I Ask God For:

Ioday's Intention: Today I Release _____
                                               And Hope To Gain

Today's Relationship With   I Am Excited About:

_____

Looks Like: I Promise Myself:

My Next Partner Will:

Tatiana's Personal Note: Upgrade your reality to match your dreams.

Date: Mood:

Today I Affirm: My Future Relationship Will Feel:

Today I Feel: Today I Ask God For:

Today's Intention: Today I Release _____
                                         And Hope To Gain

Today's Relationship With   I Am Excited About:

_____

Looks Like: I Promise Myself:

My Next Partner Will:

Tatiana's Personal Note: If you are worth pursuing, stop asking why it's taking time.

254

BELIEVE

IN YOUR

DOPENESS

I WIN BECAUSE I KEEP GOING

Date:

Mood:

Today I Affirm:

My Future Relationship Will Feel:

Today I Feel:

Today I Ask God For:

Today's Intention:

Today I Release _____
And Hope To Gain

Today's Relationship With

I Am Excited About:

_____

Looks Like:

I Promise Myself:

My Next Partner Will:

Tatiana's Personal Note: Be okay with taking a chance on love.

Date:

Today I Affirm:

Today I Feel:

Today's Intention:

Today's Relationship With

_____

Looks Like:

My Next Partner Will:

Mood:

My Future Relationship Will Feel:

Today I Ask God For:

Today I Release _____
And Hope To Gain

I Am Excited About:

I Promise Myself:

Tatiana's Personal Note: Do not let the fear of the unknown keep you from what belongs to you.

Date:

Today I Affirm:

Today I Feel:

Today's Intention:

Today's Relationship With

_____

Looks Like:

My Next Partner Will:

Mood:

My Future Relationship Will Feel:

Today I Ask God For:

Today I Release _____
And Hope To Gain

I Am Excited About:

I Promise Myself:

Tatiana's Personal Note: Love is calling.

Date: Mood:

Today I Affirm: My Future Relationship Will Feel:

Today I Feel: Today I Ask God For:

Today's Intention: Today I Release _____
                                               And Hope To Gain

Today's Relationship With   I Am Excited About:

_____

Looks Like: I Promise Myself:

My Next Partner Will:

Tatiana's Personal Note: Be mentally and spiritually available for your future.

Date: Mood:

Today I Affirm: My Future Relationship Will Feel:

Today I Feel: Today I Ask God For:

Today's Intention: Today I Release _____
                                   And Hope To Gain

Today's Relationship With   I Am Excited About:

_____

Looks Like: I Promise Myself:

My Next Partner Will:

Tatiana's Personal Note: Your new outlook will bring in a new and exciting adventure.

261

Date: Mood:

Today I Affirm: My Future Relationship Will Feel:

Today I Feel: Today I Ask God For:

Today's Intention: Today I Release _____
                                             And Hope To Gain

Today's Relationship With   I Am Excited About:

_____

Looks Like: I Promise Myself:

My Next Partner Will:

Tatiana's Personal Note: Go ahead. Make your request for new, passionate and responsible love.

262

Date:

Today I Affirm:

Today I Feel:

Today's Intention:

Today's Relationship With

_____

Looks Like:

My Next Partner Will:

Mood:

My Future Relationship Will Feel:

Today I Ask God For:

Today I Release _____
And Hope To Gain

I Am Excited About:

I Promise Myself:

Tatiana's Personal Note: Be proud of who you are.

I DO NOT JUST LOOK LIKE LOVE. I FEEL LIKE IT TOO.

MY ABILITY TO LOVE AGAIN IS PHENOMENAL

Date: Mood:

Today I Affirm: My Future Relationship Will Feel:

Today I Feel: Today I Ask God For:

Today's Intention: Today I Release _____
                                               And Hope To Gain

Today's Relationship With   I Am Excited About:

_____

Looks Like: I Promise Myself:

My Next Partner Will:

Tatiana's Personal Note: Be hopeful about what and who is coming your way.

Date: Mood:

Today I Affirm: My Future Relationship Will Feel:

Today I Feel: Today I Ask God For:

Today's Intention: Today I Release _____
                                         And Hope To Gain

Today's Relationship With   I Am Excited About:

_____

Looks Like: I Promise Myself:

My Next Partner Will:

Tatiana's Personal Note: A simple reminder that you have not been forgotten about. God hears you.

Date: Mood:

Today I Affirm: My Future Relationship Will Feel:

Today I Feel: Today I Ask God For:

Today's Intention: Today I Release _____
                                         And Hope To Gain

Today's Relationship With   I Am Excited About:

_____

Looks Like: I Promise Myself:

My Next Partner Will:

Tatiana's Personal Note: It's okay to love again and again and again. It's called living in your spirit.

268

Date:

Today I Affirm:

Today I Feel:

Today's Intention:

Today's Relationship With

_____

Looks Like:

My Next Partner Will:

Mood:

My Future Relationship Will Feel:

Today I Ask God For:

Today I Release _____
And Hope To Gain

I Am Excited About:

I Promise Myself:

Tatiana's Personal Note: It's time to do some new things. Go somewhere different and try something new.

Date: Mood:

Today I Affirm: My Future Relationship Will Feel:

Today I Feel: Today I Ask God For:

Today's Intention: Today I Release _____
                                         And Hope To Gain

Today's Relationship With   I Am Excited About:

_____

Looks Like: I Promise Myself:

My Next Partner Will:

Tatiana's Personal Note: Someone is waiting on you to notice the beauty within yourself.

I WILL NOT ALLOW SOMEONE TO NEGATIVELY CHANGE MY DEFINITION OF

I CAN TREAT HIM LIKE A KING, BECAUSE I KNOW HOW TO TREAT MYSELF LIKE A QUEEN.

Date:

Today I Affirm:

Today I Feel:

Today's Intention:

Today's Relationship With

_____

Looks Like:

My Next Partner Will:

Mood:

My Future Relationship Will Feel:

Today I Ask God For:

Today I Release _____
And Hope To Gain

I Am Excited About:

I Promise Myself:

Tatiana's Personal Note: The possibilities of love is what makes life amazing. It can happen at anytime.

Date:

Today I Affirm:

Today I Feel:

Today's Intention:

Today's Relationship With

_____

Looks Like:

My Next Partner Will:

Mood:

My Future Relationship Will Feel:

Today I Ask God For:

Today I Release _____
And Hope To Gain

I Am Excited About:

I Promise Myself:

Tatiana's Personal Note: Even when you do not feel love, remember that a lot of things that you have and are is because of love.

Date:

Today I Affirm:

Today I Feel:

Today's Intention:

Today's Relationship With

_____

Looks Like:

My Next Partner Will:

Mood:

My Future Relationship Will Feel:

Today I Ask God For:

Today I Release _____
And Hope To Gain

I Am Excited About:

I Promise Myself:

Tatiana's Personal Note: When you're loved correctly you can feel it. Stop fighting for something you can't feel.

Date:

Today I Affirm:

Today I Feel:

Today's Intention:

Today's Relationship With

_____

Looks Like:

My Next Partner Will:

Mood:

My Future Relationship Will Feel:

Today I Ask God For:

Today I Release _____
And Hope To Gain

I Am Excited About:

I Promise Myself:

Tatiana's Personal Note: Embrace this season in your life as it is preparing you for the next amazing level.

Date: Mood:

Today I Affirm: My Future Relationship Will Feel:

Today I Feel: Today I Ask God For:

Today's Intention: Today I Release _____
                                               And Hope To Gain

Today's Relationship With   I Am Excited About:

_____

Looks Like: I Promise Myself:

My Next Partner Will:

Tatiana's Personal Note: Promise yourself to be present and enjoy what many don't take the time to see.

Date:

Today I Affirm:

Today I Feel:

Today's Intention:

Today's Relationship With

_____

Looks Like:

My Next Partner Will:

Mood:

My Future Relationship Will Feel:

Today I Ask God For:

Today I Release _____
And Hope To Gain

I Am Excited About:

I Promise Myself:

Tatiana's Personal Note: Feel the love that you want. Daily.

278

Date:

Mood:

Today I Affirm:

My Future Relationship Will Feel:

Today I Feel:

Today I Ask God For:

Today's Intention:

Today I Release _____
And Hope To Gain

Today's Relationship With

I Am Excited About:

_____

Looks Like:

I Promise Myself:

My Next Partner Will:

Tatiana's Personal Note: You'll notice that the greatest moments in your life were never forced.

Date: Mood:

Today I Affirm: My Future Relationship Will Feel:

Today I Feel: Today I Ask God For:

Today's Intention: Today I Release _____
                                         And Hope To Gain

Today's Relationship With   I Am Excited About:

_____

Looks Like: I Promise Myself:

My Next Partner Will:

Tatiana's Personal Note: Your love towards others is needed.

SHE WAS AMAZING BECAUSE SHE ALWAYS MADE YOU FEEL SOMETHING.

ME. THE MOST BEAUTIFUL WOMAN I KNOW.

Date: Mood:

Today I Affirm: My Future Relationship Will Feel:

Today I Feel: Today I Ask God For:

Today's Intention: Today I Release _____
                                         And Hope To Gain

Today's Relationship With   I Am Excited About:

_____

Looks Like: I Promise Myself:

My Next Partner Will:

Tatiana's Personal Note: Be the light even when everyone else wants to live in darkness.

283

Date:

Today I Affirm:

Today I Feel:

Today's Intention:

Today's Relationship With

_____

Looks Like:

My Next Partner Will:

Mood:

My Future Relationship Will Feel:

Today I Ask God For:

Today I Release _____
And Hope To Gain

I Am Excited About:

I Promise Myself:

Tatiana's Personal Note: To feel continuous love, always stay connected to God.

Date:

Today I Affirm:

Today I Feel:

Today's Intention:

Today's Relationship With

_____

Looks Like:

My Next Partner Will:

Mood:

My Future Relationship Will Feel:

Today I Ask God For:

Today I Release _____
And Hope To Gain

I Am Excited About:

I Promise Myself:

Tatiana's Personal Note: Give yourself permission to be loved.

Date: Mood:

Today I Affirm: My Future Relationship Will Feel:

Today I Feel: Today I Ask God For:

Today's Intention: Today I Release _____
                                         And Hope To Gain

Today's Relationship With   I Am Excited About:

_____

Looks Like: I Promise Myself:

My Next Partner Will:

Tatiana's Personal Note: You deserve effort and consistency. You deserve friendship and love.

Date:

Today I Affirm:

Today I Feel:

Today's Intention:

Today's Relationship With

_____

Looks Like:

My Next Partner Will:

Mood:

My Future Relationship Will Feel:

Today I Ask God For:

Today I Release _____
And Hope To Gain

I Am Excited About:

I Promise Myself:

Tatiana's Personal Note: Start believing love belongs to you because love is you.

Date:

Today I Affirm:

Today I Feel:

Today's Intention:

Today's Relationship With

_____

Looks Like:

My Next Partner Will:

Mood:

My Future Relationship Will Feel:

Today I Ask God For:

Today I Release _____

And Hope To Gain

I Am Excited About:

I Promise Myself:

Tatiana's Personal Note: Allow others to love you. Every part of you.

Date:

Today I Affirm:

Today I Feel:

Today's Intention:

Today's Relationship With

_____

Looks Like:

My Next Partner Will:

Mood:

My Future Relationship Will Feel:

Today I Ask God For:

Today I Release _____
And Hope To Gain

I Am Excited About:

I Promise Myself:

Tatiana's Personal Note: Find your peace and stay there.

IN THIS EXACT MOMENT, I HAVE ACCEPTED MYSELF.

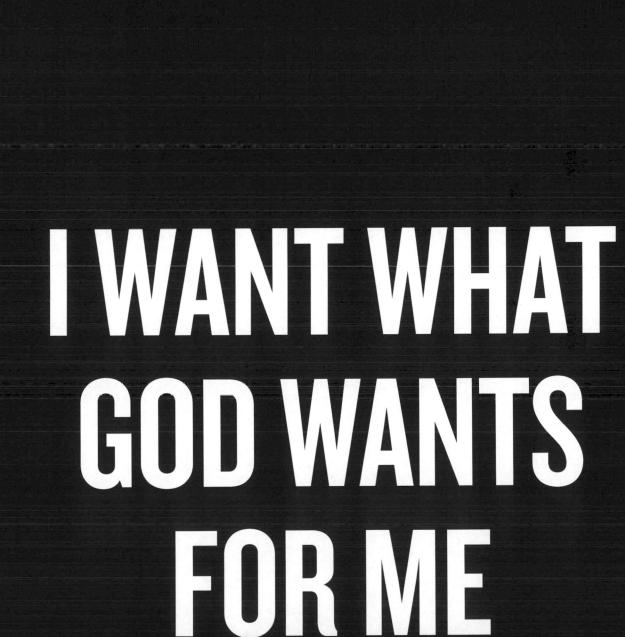

Date:

Today I Affirm:

Today I Feel:

Today's Intention:

Today's Relationship With

_____

Looks Like:

My Next Partner Will:

Mood:

My Future Relationship Will Feel:

Today I Ask God For:

Today I Release _____
And Hope To Gain

I Am Excited About:

I Promise Myself:

Tatiana's Personal Note: You can't hide from love.

Date:

Today I Affirm:

Today I Feel:

Today's Intention:

Today's Relationship With

_____

Looks Like:

My Next Partner Will:

Mood:

My Future Relationship Will Feel:

Today I Ask God For:

Today I Release _____
And Hope To Gain

I Am Excited About:

I Promise Myself:

Tatiana's Personal Note: You can see love through actions.

Date:

Today I Affirm:

Today I Feel:

Today's Intention:

Today's Relationship With

_____

Looks Like:

My Next Partner Will:

Mood:

My Future Relationship Will Feel:

Today I Ask God For:

Today I Release _____
And Hope To Gain

I Am Excited About:

I Promise Myself:

Tatiana's Personal Note: No longer afraid of love.

Date: Mood:

Today I Affirm: My Future Relationship Will Feel:

Today I Feel: Today I Ask God For:

Today's Intention: Today I Release _____
                                           And Hope To Gain

Today's Relationship With   I Am Excited About:

_____

Looks Like: I Promise Myself:

My Next Partner Will:

Tatiana's Personal Note: It feels good to be in the process of healing.

Date: Mood:

Today I Affirm: My Future Relationship Will Feel:

Today I Feel: Today I Ask God For:

Today's Intention: Today I Release _____
                                             And Hope To Gain

Today's Relationship With   I Am Excited About:

_____

Looks Like: I Promise Myself:

My Next Partner Will:

Tatiana's Personal Note: No longer will you lose yourself when loving someone else.

Date:

Today I Affirm:

Today I Feel:

Today's Intention:

Today's Relationship With

_____

Looks Like:

My Next Partner Will:

Mood:

My Future Relationship Will Feel:

Today I Ask God For:

Today I Release _____
And Hope To Gain

I Am Excited About:

I Promise Myself:

Tatiana's Personal Note: Use your words to create your new life.

297

Date: Mood:

Today I Affirm: My Future Relationship Will Feel:

Today I Feel: Today I Ask God For:

Today's Intention: Today I Release _____
                                               And Hope To Gain

Today's Relationship With   I Am Excited About:

_____

Looks Like: I Promise Myself:

My Next Partner Will:

Tatiana's Personal Note: The relationship you have with yourself and God is a clear indication of the kind of relationship you will have with your next love.

Date:

Today I Affirm:

Today I Feel:

Today's Intention:

Today's Relationship With

_____

Looks Like:

My Next Partner Will:

Mood:

My Future Relationship Will Feel:

Today I Ask God For:

Today I Release _____
And Hope To Gain

I Am Excited About:

I Promise Myself:

Tatiana's Personal Note: Your prayers get attention.

THERE IS MORE THAN ENOUGH LOVE TO LAST A MILLION LIFETIMES.
— I PROMISE

Date: Mood:

Today I Affirm: My Future Relationship Will Feel:

Today I Feel: Today I Ask God For:

Today's Intention: Today I Release _____
                                       And Hope To Gain

Today's Relationship With   I Am Excited About:

_____

Looks Like: I Promise Myself:

My Next Partner Will:

Tatiana's Personal Note: Others will see you the way you see yourself.

Date: Mood:

Today I Affirm: My Future Relationship Will Feel:

Today I Feel: Today I Ask God For:

Today's Intention: Today I Release _____
And Hope To Gain

Today's Relationship With   I Am Excited About:

_____

Looks Like: I Promise Myself:

My Next Partner Will:

Tatiana's Personal Note: Because you love yourself, he will love you too.

303

Date: Mood:

Today I Affirm: My Future Relationship Will Feel:

Today I Feel: Today I Ask God For:

Today's Intention: Today I Release _____
                                               And Hope To Gain

Today's Relationship With   I Am Excited About:

_____

Looks Like: I Promise Myself:

My Next Partner Will:

Tatiana's Personal Note: Stay faithful in believing in new love.

Date: Mood:

Today I Affirm: My Future Relationship Will Feel:

Today I Feel: Today I Ask God For:

Today's Intention: Today I Release _____
                                       And Hope To Gain

Today's Relationship With   I Am Excited About:

_____

Looks Like: I Promise Myself:

My Next Partner Will:

Tatiana's Personal Note: True and unconditional love replenishes and forgives.

Date: Mood:

Today I Affirm: My Future Relationship Will Feel:

Today I Feel: Today I Ask God For:

Today's Intention: Today I Release _____
                                         And Hope To Gain

Today's Relationship With   I Am Excited About:

_____

Looks Like: I Promise Myself:

My Next Partner Will:

Tatiana's Personal Note: Be okay with those not receptive to your love. Some may not know how to respond to that. Don't let that stop you from loving.

Date: Mood:

Today I Affirm: My Future Relationship Will Feel:

Today I Feel: Today I Ask God For:

Today's Intention: Today I Release _____
                                               And Hope To Gain

Today's Relationship With   I Am Excited About:

_____

Looks Like: I Promise Myself:

My Next Partner Will:

Tatiana's Personal Note: Protect your space. Protect your peace.

Date: Mood:

Today I Affirm: My Future Relationship Will Feel:

Today I Feel: Today I Ask God For:

Today's Intention: Today I Release _____
                                         And Hope To Gain

Today's Relationship With   I Am Excited About:

_____

Looks Like: I Promise Myself:

My Next Partner Will:

Tatiana's Personal Note: Do everything out of love. Even if others don't operate out of love, make sure you do.

Date: Mood:

Today I Affirm: My Future Relationship Will Feel:

Today I Feel: Today I Ask God For:

Today's Intention: Today I Release _____
                                               And Hope To Gain

Today's Relationship With   I Am Excited About:

_____

Looks Like: I Promise Myself:

My Next Partner Will:

Tatiana's Personal Note: You have so much more levels to experience.

I HAVE ACCEPTED MYSELF AND SOON THE RIGHT PERSON WILL MORE THAN ACCEPT ME TOO.

LOVE IS PATIENT, LOVE IS KIND. IT DOES NOT ENVY, IT DOES NOT BOAST, IT IS NOT PROUD. IT DOES NOT DISHONOR OTHERS, IT IS NOT SELF-SEEKING, IT IS NOT EASILY ANGERED, IT KEEPS NO RECORD OF WRONGS. LOVE DOES NOT DELIGHT IN EVIL BUT REJOICES WITH THE TRUTH. IT ALWAYS PROTECTS, ALWAYS TRUSTS, ALWAYS HOPES, ALWAYS PERSEVERES.

- I CORINTHIANS 13:4-7

Date:

Today I Affirm:

Today I Feel:

Today's Intention:

Today's Relationship With

_____

Looks Like:

My Next Partner Will:

Mood:

My Future Relationship Will Feel:

Today I Ask God For:

Today I Release _____
And Hope To Gain

I Am Excited About:

I Promise Myself:

Tatiana's Personal Note: Show the world how amazing you are.

Date:

Today I Affirm:

Today I Feel:

Today's Intention:

Today's Relationship With

_____

Looks Like:

My Next Partner Will:

Mood:

My Future Relationship Will Feel:

Today I Ask God For:

Today I Release _____
And Hope To Gain

I Am Excited About:

I Promise Myself:

Tatiana's Personal Note: You are filled with favor. Others see it, so should you.

313

Date:

Today I Affirm:

Today I Feel:

Today's Intention:

Today's Relationship With

_____

Looks Like:

My Next Partner Will:

Mood:

My Future Relationship Will Feel:

Today I Ask God For:

Today I Release _____
And Hope To Gain

I Am Excited About:

I Promise Myself:

Tatiana's Personal Note: Get ready for your love breakthrough.

Date:

Today I Affirm:

Today I Feel:

Today's Intention:

Today's Relationship With

_____

Looks Like:

My Next Partner Will:

Mood:

My Future Relationship Will Feel:

Today I Ask God For:

Today I Release _____
And Hope To Gain

I Am Excited About:

I Promise Myself:

Tatiana's Personal Note: You should no longer settle for anyone to half love you.

Date:

Today I Affirm:

Today I Feel:

Today's Intention:

Today's Relationship With

_____

Looks Like:

My Next Partner Will:

Mood:

My Future Relationship Will Feel:

Today I Ask God For:

Today I Release _____
And Hope To Gain

I Am Excited About:

I Promise Myself:

Tatiana's Personal Note: You are as amazing as you say you are.

Date: Mood:

Today I Affirm: My Future Relationship Will Feel:

Today I Feel: Today I Ask God For:

Today's Intention: Today I Release _____
                                               And Hope To Gain

Today's Relationship With   I Am Excited About:

_____

Looks Like: I Promise Myself:

My Next Partner Will:

Tatiana's Personal Note: A lot may have changed, but things could change for the better.

Date:

Today I Affirm:

Today I Feel:

Today's Intention:

Today's Relationship With

_____

Looks Like:

My Next Partner Will:

Mood:

My Future Relationship Will Feel:

Today I Ask God For:

Today I Release _____
And Hope To Gain

I Am Excited About:

I Promise Myself:

Tatiana's Personal Note: Don't ever worry about how bright your light is.

Date: Mood:

Today I Affirm: My Future Relationship Will Feel:

Today I Feel: Today I Ask God For:

Today's Intention: Today I Release _____
                                         And Hope To Gain

Today's Relationship With   I Am Excited About:

_____

Looks Like: I Promise Myself:

My Next Partner Will:

Tatiana's Personal Note: Always believe love will make its way to you.

Date: Mood:

Today I Affirm: My Future Relationship Will Feel:

Today I Feel: Today I Ask God For:

Today's Intention: Today I Release _____
                                               And Hope To Gain

Today's Relationship With   I Am Excited About:

_____

Looks Like: I Promise Myself:

My Next Partner Will:

Tatiana's Personal Note: Don't ever under-estimate the power of your love.

SAYING YES TO ANYTHING THAT MAKES ME HAPPY AND HELPS ME TO GROW

BECAUSE OF GOD, I AM LOVED..... ALWAYS. IN ALL WAYS.

Date: Mood:

Today I Affirm: My Future Relationship Will Feel:

Today I Feel: Today I Ask God For:

Today's Intention: Today I Release _____
                                         And Hope To Gain

Today's Relationship With   I Am Excited About:

_____

Looks Like: I Promise Myself:

My Next Partner Will:

Tatiana's Personal Note: It's okay to fall in love …. all over again.

Made in the USA
Columbia, SC
09 December 2017